CONTENTS

CHAPTER 1	6
CHAPTER 2	19
CHAPTER 3	26
CHAPTER 4	48
CHAPTER 5	55
CHAPTER 6	66
CHAPTER 7	82
CHAPTER 8	92
CHAPTER 9	102
CHAPTER 10	110

DAVE MARSHALL

FOR THE PUBLIC WHO DESERVE BETTER

1. Crime Fighters: Policing in the 1990's
2. Intelligence Led Policing, Performance Monitoring, and Some Unintended Consequences
3. Diversity, Equity, and Inclusion. The Cancellation Begins
4. End of the Policing Mission: What Are the Police For?
5. Politics and Police Leadership: One step forward For Politics, Two Steps Back for Leadership
6. Sexists, Racists, and Misogynists: The Cancellation Takes Hold
7. When it Hits the Fan, Experience Counts
8. The College of Policing: A Unique Experience
9. What About the Public?
10. Sir Robert Peel. A Final Word

Introduction

Once the envy of the world, the British Police service is now in complete freefall. Public confidence is at an all-time low, serious crime in many parts of the country is on the rise, and more police forces than at any point in history have been placed into 'special measures' by the police inspectorate, including the once iconic but now scandal-ridden Metropolitan Police Service. Police leadership appears completely inept, and those at the top of policing seem to be either incapable or unwilling to reignite the conventional law enforcement, crime fighting mission that the law-abiding majority expect of its police. The ability to engage in proper policing and to achieve even the most basic of public expectations is a seemingly impossible endeavour for many of our police forces, with confidence in policing now rock bottom. Police officers seemingly spend as much time and commitment expressing a social conscience nowadays through woke-fuelled virtue signalling activity than they do deterring crime and catching criminals. But how did our police service find itself in such a sorry state? What caused Sir Robert Peel's iconic model of 'policing by consent' go from a shining beacon of democratic policing to the dire situation in which it currently now exists.

In this book, criminologist and former senior police officer, Dave Marshall, examines the past 30 years of British Policing. Using a combination of personal experience and critical analysis, Marshall outlines how through a blinkered over-indulgence in the woke agenda, diversity, equality, and inclusion policies, while pandering to the divisive ideology of identity politics, the police service effectively cancelled its much loved and respected British Bobby. Through his analysis, the author explores the seminal moments and key decisions that caused British policing to spiral into such an unrecognisable and poorly regarded public service, one riddled with incompetence, repeated allegations of wrongdoing, discrimination, with serious questions frequently now asked about its legitimacy and concerns over dwindling public trust. The subject of police leadership is examined in detail, and the question explored as to precisely why so many in the modern police hierarchy appear so woefully ill-equipped, incapable, or unwilling to deliver effective policing for their communities.

About the Author

Dave Marshall is a former senior police officer who served in various parts of the UK and in range of diverse and challenging operational policing and command roles. Over his thirty-year career, Dave led the response to many high-profile public order operations, significant major incidents, and civil emergencies. He is passionate about police wellbeing and was actively involved in the development of national wellbeing and suicide prevention strategies. Dave's last role in policing was at the College of Policing where he led nationally on police performance improvement, supporting forces placed by the police inspectorate into 'special measures. On leaving the police service, he has pursued his academic interests and is now a university lecturer in criminology and criminal justice.

CHAPTER 1

Crime Fighters: Policing in the 1990's

I began my police career at the age of 17 as Cadet 0792 in the former Grampian Police Force (now part of the Police Service of Scotland) on 7th of September 1992. Joining the police had been my childhood ambition, and I was over the moon to receive the letter in the post confirming that I had been successful in my application to become one of only 12 police cadets to be recruited that year. I still have that letter. The purpose of annually recruiting police cadets to the force was to ensure a guaranteed recruitment pipeline existed to help supplement conventional police recruitment processes. This ensured a minimum level of available police recruits each year, put in place at a time when applications to join the police could never be guaranteed, particularly in the north east of Scotland where jobs in the offshore oil and fishing industries were plentiful, and were generally well paid. Cadets were appointed to the force between the ages of 16 and a half and 17 and a half years old, and if successful in their cadetship were appointed to the office of constable on the intake nearest to their 18 and a half birthday (for some reason the police service used the 'and a half' thing in those days).

The cadet training programme was physically challenging, where regular fitness sessions were undertaken, hillwalking expeditions once a month at all times of the year in the stunning Grampian countryside, and a Duke of Edinburgh programme of volunteering in a number of outside institutions to gain vital life experience. It was a process of discipline, camaraderie, and of instilling public service and community awareness into young people who would shortly don the police uniform and patrol the streets as newly appointed constables. It was an effective programme, one that in the main turned out fit, disciplined young police officers, ready for a life of public service and commitment to their chosen profession. Following two separate training courses at the Scottish Police College, Tulliallan Castle, Kincardineshire, which, in those days was run very much along military lines, followed by a two-year probationary period I would become a fully-fledged policeman. Towards the end of the Cadet programme, each of us was given an operational posting, mine being to Peterhead in the north-east of the region.

The Scottish Police College

As a Police Cadet, I had already been well prepared on what to expect in advance of our formal training at Tulliallan Castle, the training college for all of Scotland's police forces including the British Transport Police, and now the Headquarters of Scotland's national police service. We had been on a few visits to Tulliallan and so became familiar with its structures and training processes prior to commencing our formal police training. This was not a place for the faint hearted in the early 1990's. Discipline was intense, recruits were accommodated 12 to a dormitory with complete strangers, and essentially you surrendered your life outside of police training for the entire period of your time there, 10 weeks in the first year, and eight weeks in the second. The physical fitness regime was tough, and I vividly recall running with benches from the gym hall on our backs through the forest in late autumn and winter, in freezing temperatures with snow and ice covering the ground and with many of my course mates losing their breakfast on the aptly named 'rice crispy hill' during early morning training sessions. The instructors at the College were all serving police sergeants, most of whom were themselves highly experienced police officers. They commanded respect and drilled into new recruits the highest level of standards, discipline, and appearance. Uniforms had to be properly pressed and shoes bulled. For new police recruits, the experience was like a prolonged job interview; you could never fully relax, were never off duty, and your character was constantly being assessed and tested to ensure your continued suitability and aptitude for the police constable role. It was also designed to ensure that as new recruits, we fully understood our place in the pecking order. And that is exactly as it should be. New police recruits were without exception in those days first and foremost trained and deployed as front-line operational officers for a minimum of two years. Discipline and adherence to orders and instruction was then and is now a vital attribute for police officers. The public does not distinguish between an officer who may have spent five years in the force from one who has spent just five minutes, and so newly qualified police officers must be expected to respond as efficiently and decisively in any given situation no matter that it might be their first day on the beat. The ability to receive and discharge orders from senior colleagues has always been critical in the performance of the role, and the Scottish Police College did a fine job of instilling this concept.

In those days, Tulliallan was run very much akin to a military training establishment. Recruits were accommodated in shared dormitories which had to be kept utterly pristine at all times, male and female recruits were accommodated separately, and both sexes warned in no uncertain terms that any 'mixing' discovered in dormitories would result in recruits being expelled from Tulliallan and returned back to their respective police force; effectively they would be sacked. There were strong rumours that bromide was mixed into the recruit's tea to help suppress their sexual appetite, a rumour that I must confess I never did get to the bottom of. But as an urban myth it was nonetheless convincing to an impressionable 18-year-old. I won't divulge whether I engaged in any such undetected 'mixing' endeavours.

Life at Tulliallan was tough, and most certainly geared towards pushing recruits to their very limits in respect of personal resilience and character. Physical fitness regimes were intense, as were the various classes and examinations on legal disciplines.

Not everyone made it to the end of the course, and from my experience those married and especially with children struggled most as the course was entirely residential Monday to Friday. Weekends were generally spent studying and getting uniform and kit ready for the following week. The experience was all consuming but looking back it was most definitely worthwhile. The pass out parade at the end of the course was an occasion where friends and family would come to Tulliallan and see their loved ones in their shiny new police uniforms (full tunic dress in those days and not the cheap looking black lycra style tops we see now!) marching impressively around the parade square accompanied by one of the police pipe bands. It was a proud moment for all concerned including the training staff who would bid farewell to their charges as they went forth and discovered the realities of operational police work.

My Introduction to Policing

My first operational shift as a Police Constable was on Christmas Day 1993 commencing at 6.00pm. I walked into Peterhead police station which I was fortunately already familiar with and was to join the same team and Sergeant I had been attached to as a Police Cadet. I had just changed into my nicely pressed uniform when I heard a commotion from the cell block which was adjacent to the male changing rooms. I diligently charged through to see an open cell door and a rather large male prisoner being only marginally restrained by two of my colleagues. He had been arrested earlier that day after officers responded to a domestic incident at his home address where on their arrival, he threatened to shoot them with his shotgun. Fortunately, a swift and effective baton strike by one of the attending officers prevented him from fetching his gun and so thankfully he was unable to achieve that ambition. Regardless, he had struggled violently with the officers during the arrest and had continued to do so while in custody. I entered the cell and got stuck in, joining the melee of thrashing arms and legs. Between us we eventually managed to restrain the prisoner long enough for him to be properly searched before rapidly exiting the cell. Welcome back I thought.

Christmas is an interesting time for policing. While most people relax at home enjoying a few festive drinks and watching repeats of Gavin and Stacey and The Two Ronnie's, there are always plenty of calls coming into police control rooms, normally domestic related and invariably involving over consumption of alcohol. My first shift on Christmas Day 1993 was a busy one. A colleague and I were called to a domestic disturbance whereby a man had reportedly smashed up his partners car and was now marauding about the streets bare chested. On arrival at the address the street itself was eerily quiet. There were certainly no signs of a disturbance described to us by the control room dispatcher. It was around 11pm and most festivities were winding down in the households of the Peterhead suburbs. All appeared normal. Then we saw the car which, as reported, had every piece of glass smashed through, every window and both front and rear windscreens. No sooner had we started to inspect the vehicle and its damage than said bare chested man, seemingly out of nowhere, started walking quickly towards us brandishing a broken vodka bottle in a threatening manner. Now in those days, our only method of protection was a short wooden baton concealed in a pocket in your trouser leg and a pair of handcuffs. There was no body armour, extendable metal batons, pepper spray or tasers. No 24-hour armed response capability existed in the Grampian force in those days. Rather, firearms officers were called out and armed if needs be. So, we did what cops always did in those days in situations of possible violence. There was no messing about, no five-step appeal process to try and de-escalate the situation, we simply took a hold of him, disarmed him of his bottle, and after a short scuffle had him in cuffs and in the back of our Vauxhall Astra estate tussled up like a Christmas turkey. Nowadays I can imagine how this scenario would likely play out. There would be batons drawn, pepper spray used, or even a taser discharged. But this was the 1990's and no such protection existed. Cops just needed to get hands on and hope for the best. Standing back and assessing the risks posed by the situation or even waiting for back-up (often there was no back-up) was simply not an option. Witnessing police officers standing-off rather than deal with a potentially violent individual also did absolutely nothing for public confidence or reassurance. So, getting stuck in was the default response whatever the perceived danger. And in every single situation this is what we did regardless of risk, how big the 'other guy' was, or if a weapon was present.

Self-defence training had consisted of a grand total of two days at Tulliallan in the first 10 weeks where some impossible to execute arm holds were demonstrated along with minimal instruction on how to use your baton - simply don't hit them on the head and keep it out of sight being the extent of that particular lesson. The application of chain-link handcuffs was also demonstrated. Much more time was spent on swimming instruction and lifesaving as well as marching around the parade square than there was on self-defence preparation. And nobody remotely questioned this. Police recruits of that era were expected to be of a calibre whereby they were physically able to protect themselves without resorting to weapons. Minimum height regulations were still in place for recruits (5'8" for men and 5'4" for women) and for very good reason, and physical fitness designed to increase strength and stamina were key parts of the training regime. It was of no surprise then that when faced with violent confrontations – and I experienced many such confrontations in my first decade of service – that cops reverted to what they knew and what worked best for them and generally did so confidently. And more often than not, it got the job done with minimal fuss or injury to either side of the confrontation.

I was to spend the next seven years at Peterhead, and looking back perhaps with some rose-tinted eyewear, those were hands down the best days of my police career. I worked with some truly outstanding police officers, the sense of camaraderie was palpable, and leadership consisted generally of experienced police officers who had seen and done it themselves. Policing was also significantly less complex in those days. The 'mission' was clear and understood without the need for the publication of uninspiring mission statements or jazzy organisational vision posters plastered all over police premises as we see nowadays (even one cannot escape such propaganda messages when claiming the sanctuary of a bathroom stall in some places). Lock up the bad people and look after the good people. That was all you needed to understand, and those who joined the profession in those days understood that basic but critical tenant of police work very well. I do not in any way understate how tough operational policing was in those days, especially in a town like Peterhead, where the divide between rich and poor was stark, and the heroin trade of the 1990's was quickly starting to take hold. Many towns and cities across the UK mirrored this policing demographic. I simply mean that policing was discharged in a less complex manner, with far less political interference, and frontline officers were treated like professionals where their operational decision-making and discretion was seldom questioned. When dispatched by the sergeant at the beginning of our tour of duty, we were seldom explicitly told what to do or where to patrol unless a specific call needed attended to or a particular operation or initiative was taking place. We were trusted to know our patch, to patrol the areas that were of greatest significance and concern, and to conduct our business in a proactive manner, one that targeted known wrongdoers, letting them know who was in charge. We, as representatives of the law-abiding public, were in charge, and the criminals needed to know that. We also seldom got involved in the work of other agencies such as health (particularly mental health), social services or other functions which involved people. We were the police, and our core mission was to enforce the law. If we felt that other agencies were better placed, then we simply ensured that they discharged their own respective functions. Rarely did such non police related calls for service get as far as an operational police resource. The same certainly cannot be said in the current era. More on that topic later.

None of this is to infer that police officers of that time were individuals cut from the same cloth with little diversity in the ranks. Despite what some might claim, there was plenty of diversity in policing at that time. Police officers came from many diverse backgrounds in terms of upbringing, prior occupations, and possessed varying social attitudes. This in my view is the ultimate reflection of true diversity, not the narrower, far lower resolution version that sadly came to pass and gain obsession status amongst the upper echelons of forces in the years to come.

Square Pegs for Square Holes

As I see it, police officers were, and to some extent notwithstanding the different entry methods that now exist including direct entry inspector and superintendent schemes, still are defined in three ways. Firstly, is the career frontline police constable who has no ambition to either specialise laterally or to gain promotion. These individuals are the backbone of the service and ensure that new entrants receive a grounded exposure to operational work, imparting valuable experience to them in the process. For the first eight years of my own career this is where I saw myself remaining as I simply loved the unpredictable nature of frontline response work. I had no appetite to specialise (I had been on both CID and Traffic attachments) or to be promoted. The second category I describe as the specialists. These are officers who often from an early stage in their careers display a natural acumen to become a detective officer or to be involved in roads policing or other specialities such as public order or firearms. These officers stand out as being suited to these specialisms early on in their careers. For instance, being tenacious and competent in even the most basic of investigations as a uniformed constable shows promising detective acumen, and these officers would normally progress to the Criminal Investigation Department, sometimes even serving in that environment for their entire career. Similar with traffic officers and other uniformed specialisms.

The third, and a much smaller group in the era I commenced my own police career, are what I describe as the ladder climbers. These are individuals who, sometimes from day one, strive to get their foot on to the first rung of the promotion ladder and to keep climbing it. Advancement in the service is what drives this category more than the satisfaction of undertaking day to day police work which some view as the 'dirty work', only necessary and tolerable to get them as quickly as possible to where they want to be, normally in a comfortable office and well away from the frontline business of policing. Some do achieve this rapid promotion ambition, whilst others become frustrated that they cannot or that they are unable to do it quickly enough.

Regardless of what category you were in, generally ability and merit were overwhelmingly the determining factors. Yes, of course isolated cases of favouritism or nepotism existed in policing as they did and still do in all organisations, but this was less frequent and normally quickly uncovered as the individual would simply not be suited to their new role or promotion if shoe-horned into it. However, as a rule, those who occupied specific specialised roles in policing were generally very well suited to them. Detectives could detect, frontline officers could effectively discharge day to day policing for communities, and leaders could normally lead, even the ladder climbers who much as some tried could never completely avoid the basic operational exposure they required. There were no internal equity targets, no talk of 'diversity optics', just an accepted system of square pegs into square holes. This system of merit and suitability also better served the public who ultimately even now I am convinced care far less about the protected characteristics of a police officer and considerably more about their effectiveness and competence to do the job.

The 1990's was an era where police officers felt much more confident and self-assured to get on with their job. By which I mean they possessed the correct training, skills, behaviours, and physical capability to discharge the office of constable. They also knew that for the most part, they had the support of the public and so the notion of policing by consent (perhaps felt more in a subliminal rather than in an explicit sense to a wet behind the ears cop like me) was still alive and well. Just as important, they knew they had the support of the organisation itself behind them 99% of the time. For the most part, your bosses would back you for the decisions you made providing these were in good faith. It was always felt far better to make a decision and to get it wrong than not to make one at all. The public expect the police to act after all, often in circumstances were information is scant and levels of stress and tension are high. I'm not for one minute saying that officers who committed deliberate acts of wrongdoing or criminality were not identified and dealt with. More that mistakes made, including perhaps some excessive uses of force, whilst you undertook your role were never career-ending. There was a greater degree of tolerance and understanding by police leadership of the realities and risk which existed at the operational level and so support, and understanding was generally evident.

I had my fair share of interactions with the Grampian Police Complaints and Discipline Department (now having the far softer designation of Professional Standards Department) in my time as a front-line officer. These were normally complaints relating to use of force considered excessive, allegations of incivility, or of stopping and searching the same individual multiple times, normally known drug users. On every occasion, a proportionate disciplinary investigation was undertaken, and on all occasions, I was cleared of wrongdoing. I didn't have sleepless nights because I knew that by and large the organisation, even the rubber-heelers of complaints and discipline, understood the realities of frontline police work. Complaints were in some respects an occupational hazard particularly for those of us who got intrusive with our local criminal fraternity. And that reality entailed on occasions being less than civil to the clientele, often using profanities, and sometimes having to make use of force judgements rapidly and without the benefit of hindsight. Rarely did you second guess your judgement or decision-making as to do so, especially in high-stress and potentially volatile circumstances could be dangerous. Therefore, most cops stepped forward rather than back, even when faced with extreme violence or the risk of violence.

I vividly recall one sleepy Tuesday early shift in Peterhead when I was single crewed on mobile patrol and was alerted to a report of an armed robbery which had only just occurred at a nearby post office. A description of the perpetrator was provided, including the vehicle he was driving and his possible direction of travel. He was said to be armed with a sawn-off shotgun, the firearm of choice in those days for bank robbers. I proceeded in my patrol car to the nearby bypass road and parked up in some hope that I might intercept the vehicle. As I've said, there was no armed response capability in the force in those days and so we, the unarmed front line was it. I was only there for a few minutes when a vehicle matching the description passed by the control room came into view with one male occupant on board. I brought my police car in behind the vehicle, advised the control room of the situation, and engaged a vehicle stop by flashing the blue lights and sounding the siren. The vehicle stopped. As I cautiously alighted my vehicle and approached the stationary suspect vehicle, the male driver got out and started walking towards me. He didn't appear to be armed. This is what I mean when I talk about the need for police officers to display quick time, high pressure decision-making. Here I had a vehicle, matching the description of the suspect vehicle, with a lone male occupant, and coming from the area where the robbery had occurred. I literally had seconds to determine my course of action, to dither or delay could see me lying dead with a bullet in me at the roadside. So, I took hold of the guy, spun him around and placed him face down onto the bonnet of my police car and slapped my handcuffs on him, advising him that I was detaining him on suspicion of armed robbery. With the suspect securely cuffed and in the back of my car, I undertook a cursory search of his vehicle. I found no shotgun, no bag of cash, or indeed anything else obviously incriminating. All I discovered was a pair of overalls and a map of the area in the boot of his car. Had I made a mistake, had I been overzealous in detaining this man who appeared very mild mannered indeed with no resistance given by him whatsoever.

On the contrary, on seeing me parked up in my marked patrol car on the bypass road he had hastily thrown the shotgun (thankfully!) and stolen money out of his car window. These were soon located by another unit who came to assist me. The overalls had been used in the commission of the robbery which he had removed prior to making his getaway, and the map was needed to locate the rural post office location he had chosen. Some months later I gave evidence at the High Court after which the male was found guilty and given a hefty custodial sentence. The point in retelling this experience is not to depict me as some sort of brave crime fighter (although it did make a good pub story over the years), but to demonstrate how a mundane Tuesday morning early shift can turn into a significant and potentially life and death incident, one requiring swift decision making. Did I make the right call? Well, nowadays it would most certainly be assessed that I did not. Unarmed officers would be ordered to step back, and a firearms response would be invoked to stop and detain the suspect. But that wasn't an option to me, I didn't have a gun and nor did any of my colleagues. So, I had to do something, even with relatively scant information and minimal personal protection and so I acted. I was a cop after all, and that's what the public expected of the police. Had I let that vehicle drive past me or failed to engage a stop I would have been seriously criticised. Instead, I received a nice letter of commendation from my superintendent and that was more than enough for me. That, and the satisfaction that I'd helped to put away a seriously bad individual. For most cops back then and even now, that is the best feeling in the world.

CHAPTER 2

Intelligence Led Policing, Performance Monitoring, and some unintended consequences

The late 1990's saw the advent of the national intelligence model (NIM), and with it the concept of 'intelligence led policing'. NIM and intelligence led policing was explained to frontline officers as the concept that with the rich use of information and intelligence would determine whether on leaving the police station to commence his or her patrol, an officer needed to turn left or right. In other words, smart crime analysis and better use of intelligence products would offer a system of predicted policing whereby in theory at least officers would use far less subjective decision making and professional judgement in how and where they spent their uncommitted patrol time. The key to success was described as ensuring intelligence submissions were generated for almost every encounter a police officer had with the public. A whole new intelligence industry was created, with the previous style of police station 'collators', normally long in service officers who knew their area exceptionally well and were entrusted with gatekeeping all the relevant intelligence on known criminals, replaced with smarter computer systems and departments of intelligence specialists. Briefings previously compiled by shift sergeants would now be completed by intelligence analysts based on current intelligence submissions and known crime trends. Sergeants now simply delivered these products as a way of assigning and deploying their shift. This was a significant change in culture and in operational policing deployment structures. No longer were officers entrusted to be in the right places at the right times but were now in fact directed where they needed to go. No longer would officers necessarily need to get to know their local criminals, now they would be told who these people were through the production of impressive 'subject profile' products. And along with this came a system of compliance monitoring with these new systems, and with it emerged the green shoots of what became to be the police performance culture which dominated most of the 2000's.

There was of course nothing wrong with these changes, and I remain a strong proponent of intelligence led policing and adherence to the national intelligence model. But the change was seismic, and as with many significant changes in policing, the process of transition was poorly executed.
Two main problems were evident. The IT systems and intelligence products were not yet fully developed, properly socialised nor sophisticated enough to replace the hitherto discretionary methods of frontline policing deployment structures. Therefore, intelligence briefings and products often made little sense to those supposedly responsible for discharging them. Predictably, this led to a lack of confidence and trust in the new processes and even to a degree of resentment. Secondly, newer generations of officers and some supervisors became blindly compliant with the new products regardless of the cynicism and often accurate critique expressed by colleagues. This led to a lack of independent critical thinking amongst some frontline officers who, rather than develop and learn from their own knowledge and experience, became totally reliant on the intelligence products supplied to dictate their day to day activities and focus. This schism created a serious disruption in effective and joined up policing, and simultaneously the reduction among many frontline officers to exercise their own professional curiosity, discretion, or interests. They simply followed the products. Leadership also did not help with this change. The new approach simply needed to be embedded at all costs, and its dissenters were to be put right. Monitoring systems were put in place to ensure compliance and for the first time ever, key performance indicators began to appear.

And none of these changes stood separately from politics. When

Blair's Labour Government took office in 1997, crime was a key election pledge with the strapline of 'tough on crime, tough on the causes of crime' and with this much more investment was quickly put into policing to deliver this key electoral pledge. The quid pro quo of course being that forces must get smarter with how they drive their daily 'business', thus the introduction of NIM which was after all essentially a business management product. Results showing improving performance needed to be demonstrated through government mandated top down objectives and targets.

The concept of intelligence led policing took a long time to take effect , partly due to systems, structures, and specialists taking time to properly embed, and partly due to the necessary socialisation, leadership, and shift in culture needed to make such changes meaningful and productive. NIM is more broadly accepted now as an established part of police business through tasking and coordinating processes and a much better awareness of the concept and processes required to drive it. However, it is a much less rigid model in today's policing structures, with greater operational discretion and flexibility built into the processes than was permitted in the early days of the concept. Intelligence led tasking of resources is now thought more as a guide to support officers in their deployments than an absolute set of instructions informing them whether they should turn left or right when they step outside the police station. In other words, it has evolved into a blend of data science and professional judgement.

The Performance Culture

Along with this important change to police business through the introduction of NIM, the regime of wider scale performance monitoring started to take hold nationwide. The Labour Government created a suite of top-down crime targets for forces which would, to some extent, determine how police forces were considered by the Home Office to be performing. Crucially, the significant investment made by the treasury into policing caused a culture whereby the government wanted to see a tangible bang for its buck, following up on its tough on crime pledge of the 1997 general election. Crime detection rates were the order of the day in this regard, and the government selected a set of crime types which they considered had caused most harm to the public including robbery and anti-social behaviour. In response to this, forces had to set in place performance management and monitoring structures whereby police commanders were, often for the very first time, held directly accountable for their areas of responsibility against the crime targets the government had set. Failure to achieve these targets was not viewed positively by those at the top of the police hierarchy, and many superintendents and chief superintendents found themselves 'developed' into other roles for failing to deliver on these targets.

The use of computer statistics – known colloquially in some law enforcement circles as COMPSTAT – drove performance management processes in many forces. Crime and Intelligence analysts were tasked with interrogating data in police IT systems to identify those areas within forces which were performing to an acceptable level, along with those whose performance statistics were less impressive against the mandated government crime targets. Ordinarily, a monthly performance meeting would take place whereby police commanders, normally superintending ranks, would be summoned to a meeting led by one of the force executive team, normally the Deputy Chief Constable, and grilled alongside peers about various aspects of their respective area's performance, including their use of tactics, and deployments. Those who were repeatedly failing to improve performance would be singled out for most attention by the force executive lead, often creating an intensely uncomfortable situation for the relevant police commander. For many, this became the single most dreaded monthly meeting, where either questioning the validity of the statistics (I did it once myself as a young chief inspector and such was the backlash never repeated it) or offering up excuses about a lack of resources was met with a sharp public rebuke. But worse than any of that was to be found that you were not on top of your crime figures be they be good, bad, or indifferent. Not knowing your business was considered a cardinal sin, and not one readily forgiven. Performance meetings became something of a blood sport, where attendees would utterly dread the spotlight being placed on them.

Some careers were certainly limited by unimpressive COMPSTAT appearances, and others were made by learning how to best play the game. In many instances an overbearing top-down leadership style and culture developed that some superintendents wrongly took forth into their own command areas to deal with their subordinates to drive local performance outcomes. This same style was being used on them after all, so why not do it to others. Many seemed completely unable or unwilling to adopt the necessary 'shock absorbers' required in senior leadership roles and simply passed on the pain to those below them in the hierarchy. The term 'what gets measured gets done' was one that entered into common police language, and it wasn't long before even the poor frontline officers, hitherto unaffected by the performance target-driven stresses and strains of their senior colleagues, began to feel this particular pain.

Dysfunctional Outcomes

Performance outcomes were eventually cascaded to frontline constable level, with individual officers now being placed under the microscope for their own contributions to the targets. The quantity of stop and searches, arrests – particularly for priority crime groups – intelligence reports submitted (regardless of the quality) were among the measures that individual officers were assessed against. And like their senior peers, many frontline officers learnt how to play this game, and play it well. One example of this was the requirement to achieve more arrests and detections for anti-social behaviour (ASB) offences. Those who know anything about policing will understand that in certain situations this amounts to shooting fish in a barrel. Visit any high street in any town or city on any Friday or Saturday night and there exists rich picking for ASB detections. Tolerance levels were in many cases lowered, with those who would normally receive only words of guidance for minor offences of drunkenness or disorderly conduct now being formally charged or even arrested in some circumstances. When ASB detection and arrest levels were starting to dip, the screws would be turned by the powers that be, and pressure applied to operational leaders at Sergeant and Inspector levels to drive this element even harder. It wasn't long before informal league tables were established between teams and police stations, these becoming formalised in certain command areas to drive a 'competitive' environment. Even the most mediocre officers learnt to play this numbers game and gain pats on the back from the hierarchy, while those who continued to believe in and invoke operational discretion were less favoured. Performance data of this type would be used when assessing officers for career development including promotion opportunities. Policing had become a numbers game and the use of discretion by police officers was getting in the way of that.

Two main difficulties arose from this approach. Firstly, it drove internal division within frontline policing teams. Until that point, there had been a consensus among the rank and file about how policing should be executed, and key to this was the right to exercise professional discretion as part of day to day policing. It also led to many dysfunctional behaviours as many officers chose to submit to the numbers game. Stop and searches shot up in number, people who would generally have been given a ticking off for minor infractions were now being unnecessarily criminalised, and the ability to exercise discretion by officers was being challenged and eroded daily. Looking back now, this situation in many ways signalled the beginning of the end. Officers were now less inclined to have to think for themselves. NIM was directing them where to go and what to do, and the performance culture and target chasing environment began the journey of eroding individual officer discretion. Some may argue that taking away discretion from frontline police officers is a good thing. After all, discretion can lead to unfortunate and inconsistent outcomes given that police officers generally operate in an environment of low managerial scrutiny as they go about their duties. As policing academic Robert Reiner describes it, in policing those at the bottom of the hierarchy possess the most amount of power over the public. However, in challenging the ability to discharge discretion, the professionalism of officers was effectively called into question and their decision-making was no longer trusted. But rather than make officers more accountable in this respect, creating an environment whereby officers had to better record, and if needs be supply rationale for their use of discretion, the approach to dilute and in some instances erode it completely was taken instead. The baby had effectively been chucked out with the bath water.

CHAPTER 3

Diversity, Equity, and Inclusion. The Cancellation Begins

Around the same time as the operational changes were beginning to take hold, several other organisational developments began to occur. Firstly, height regulations were scrapped based on the principles of diversity and inclusion. The principle reason being that those from certain ethnic minority groups, normally those from South Asia, who were generally physically smaller in stature than their indigenous British counterparts, were prevented from joining the police and that because of this, height regulations were effectively judged to constitute indirect discrimination. Therefore, it was now considered that prospective candidates for policing should no longer be automatically rejected solely because of height. Until that point, height requirements to join the police were 5'8" for men and 5'4" for women, with some forces such as the City of London Police and Northern Constabulary requiring candidates to be taller still. The Metropolitan Police were the first to ditch height restrictions in 1990 and other forces gradually followed suit over the following years. By the mid 1990's height requirements had been completely rescinded. While for many this decision was cause for celebration and considered a progressive change, many within policing, including senior officers, argued strongly against the decision, stating that policing was essentially a physical job and so a basic minimum height was needed to be effective in discharging this element of the role. I can absolutely see why many people who didn't quite achieve these height requirements would, and indeed do, make good police officers. But from my own experience, those of smaller stature are simply less able to engage in physical and volatile confrontations. That is by no means designed to be a stereotype of officers who are lacking in height. It is simply an observation over many years of being in such situations that shorter officers who lack the physical presence that height affords, especially those of slighter build, do less well in controlling violent individuals. And I mention it here because this was a significant moment in policing. It is when the diversity, equality, and inclusion (DEI) agenda began to make its rather insidious presence felt in policing.

Around the same time, fitness entry testing requirements also saw a reduction in standards. Until that point, fitness requirements for entry to policing were stringent, rightly reflecting the physically challenging elements of the role. Whilst they were tailored to consider the difference between male and female candidates, they tested all aspect of physical fitness including strength and stamina. However, once again, on examination, these high fitness standards were now also considered to be potentially prohibitive to candidates who might be less able to demonstrate them. And so, these standards too were reduced to a level where they became much easier for candidates to achieve. Again, many within policing, myself included, saw this as a regressive and unnecessary reduction in standards rather than as a progressive one.

Whilst the scrapping of height requirements and reduction of fitness testing standards for some may appear a rather innocuous event, it led to the door being wedged open for many other DEI related incursions into the world of policing, not always contributing in a positive way. In many forces, more targets were introduced, this time for the percentage of officers who should be recruited from female applicants and those from Black and Minority Ethnic (BAME) communities. In no way do I reject the notion that increasing diversity within policing is a positive thing. Of course, policing being representative of the communities it serves is in general terms a noble ambition to pursue, but this surely must be approached with a degree of realism. Some forces have stated their intention to recruit 50% female recruits. This is apparently to reflect the wider sex demographic split between men and women in contemporary society. But there is a problem with this approach. Men and women tend to pursue different career interests. Numerous studies have conclusively demonstrated that women, even in the most egalitarian of societies, tend to choose careers that are less physically confrontational, that are of a more caring or nurturing type such as primary teaching and nursing (both occupations being overwhelmingly dominated by the female sex). On the other hand, men tend to pursue careers in science and technology, the military, and yes, the police service. And there is absolutely nothing whatsoever wrong with this. Men and women are different in innumerable ways, and preferred career choice is simply one of such variables. So, to state an ambition to say recruit 50% female officers will most likely never be achieved, and even if it is, will invariably involve a requirement for bias to be engineered into recruitment processes slanted against male applicants. And this does not end with recruitment targets. In many forces, there are formal and informal equity ambitions in respect of promotion ratios, as well as progression to specialisms such as CID, firearms, and public order. And this ambition to achieve hard equity targets leads to one thing that I will state here in very simple terms. It means that selection is no longer based on merit, but on whether one possesses a desired 'protective characteristic'. It is the laziest form of what I would describe as optics-driven diversity, the low-resolution approach that fails to realise that diversity is vastly more complex. As academic Heather Mac Donald eloquently puts it, diversity is so much more than which gonads one possesses or the level of melanin in one's skin. In other words, sex and ethnic appearance is a lazy and ineffective depiction of diversity, one which fails to consider a much wider, richer, and meaningful definition.

Reducing diversity to this level may be attractive to those seeking quick wins in respect of the 'optics' it provides, but in doing so they have effectively driven down the climate of meritocracy and replaced it with a cynical form of mediocrity, one doomed to failure. And it does nothing for the service provided by the police to the public. As I've already said, most of the public call on the police at times of extreme need. They may be victims of crime, have witnessed something incredibly unpleasant, and in my experience simply want to see a police officer who is effective in their role (and yes, that includes on occasions the physical elements), is professional in how they discharge their duties, and show genuine care and empathy when needed. I am less convinced that other than in certain situations whereby female victims may rightly wish to deal with a female officer, the preference for sex, or ethnic appearance is much less important. Being suitable as a new police recruit or being competent to be a chief superintendent depends on neither sex nor skin colour. It depends on competency, ability, and aptitude. Nothing more, nothing less. But these values are sadly no longer considered as the prime requirements one needs to possess to enter the police service or to progress within it. Instead, a culture created under the guise of diversity, inclusion, and most damaging of all, equity, has mandated that those considered to possess 'privilege', normally middle aged, white, heterosexual men, need to move over and make room for the protected groups. I once heard a senior female officer I had the unfortunate experience of working alongside openly state when discussing the advancement of women in the service, 'It's **our** time now'. She then went on to characterise some of her male colleagues as being too 'male, pale and stale'.

And make no mistake, this is diversity rhetoric being played out at its worse. Those who feel they deserve to wear the badge of victimhood and entitlement simultaneously consider that they have the right to say whatever they choose when discussing the majority group, in this case white men. Furthermore, they believe that the victim badge provides them with a shield to deflect criticism. But, let's just consider the term 'male, pale, and stale'. In this one sentence we effectively use derogatory language to express sex, race, and age, all of which are protected characteristics under the Equality Act. This is language which is now frequently used and accepted by downtrodden men without challenge. I once saw in an internal police memo that white men must now consider their 'privilege' when considering diversity matters or when dealing with minority communities. At the time of writing, an Asian BBC radio presenter publicly stated that his mental health was suffering because he was 'surrounded by white people'.

Let's be clear, these are outright racist, ageist, and sexist comments regardless of which groups they are aimed at or which group is making them. But because they are being apportioned to a majority oppressor group - 'privileged white men' - they are considered as acceptable language in the struggle against sexism and misogyny. Well, they are not acceptable. You can certainly imagine if we were to reverse these terms, referring to a black female as too 'female, black and young' to perform a role, or if I said that my mental health is suffering because I'm surrounded by black people. Yes, that would rightly be considered as unacceptable language on several levels. In the police service you would likely be swiftly booted out of the organisation for even thinking such things let alone openly expressing them. This is a big problem within the current policing climate. Identity politics and an organisational obsession with diversity, inclusion and equity is rife, with many who have shot up the ranks being the biggest proponent of this liberal left political ideology.

DEI might have started out life as a set of well-intentioned and progressive ideologies, designed to make the workplace, and society in general, a fairer place for all. Of that, I have little doubt. Equality of opportunity is a laudable ambition, one designed to ensure that the same path can be traversed by all regardless of one's individual circumstances or characteristics. But equality of opportunity has morphed into the ugly concept of equality of outcome. This is an entirely different concept, designed not to create the same path, but to build in shortcuts in that path for some, and barriers for others. The path is now uneven, slanted in favour of those considered to be somehow 'underrepresented'. It allows those who display the badge of victimhood and oppression to sprint forward to positions which at best they are under qualified for, at worst unqualified for. We need look no further than at the recent case of disgraced former Harvard President, Claudine Gay, who was forced to resign amid allegations of plagiarism. Two weeks previously she had given evidence at a US congressional hearing whereby Gay refused to confirm that calling for the genocide of the Jews would be considered as harassment under Harvard's discrimination policies. Gay, the first black female to be appointed as Harvard president, possessed what could at best be described as a mediocre academic background. Nevertheless, she was appointed to one of the most prestigious academic roles on the planet. Her prior publications were limited, she did not so much as have a single book to her name, and what publications she had produced were found to contain elements of plagiarism, an offence taken so seriously in academic circles that students are often expelled when found committing it. No sooner had Gay resigned than we heard the all too predictable howls of racism being the underlying cause for her demise. There was also an immediate call by many sections of the liberal left that Gay must be replaced by another black female Harvard President. This episode starkly outlines just how warped the DEI concept has become in action. An individual appointed to the highest office in US academia for which she was by all accounts under qualified for, immediate claims of racism when she rightly decides to fall on her sword, and an assumption that her replacement must be another black female just to reset the progressive diversity dial. The one element never discussed was Gay's suitability for the role in the first place, let alone how she managed to secure it. This, for me, is an obvious example of the equality of outcome philosophy gone pathologically wrong.

And if you think this scenario is limited to US academia, you would sadly be wrong. UK policing has been similarly afflicted by this warped ideology. I have witnessed many police officers and police civilian staff appointed to positions based on their characteristics but who have been so obviously unsuitable or even under qualified for that role. Some manage to get by, normally with the help and support of those beneath them. Others have not fared so well, often quickly showing their complete lack of suitability sometimes at the direct cost of others, especially for those placed in leadership roles. I have seen this situation repeated many times, and those responsible for the appointments, normally senior officers, or their civilian counterparts, choose to ignore the ensuing chaos, choosing instead to conveniently deflect blame elsewhere. And who suffers most? The public of course. You need only look at the state of British policing. There are more forces assessed to be underperforming in even the most basic elements of policing such as investigating crime than those who are doing well. Only six out of the 43 police forces in England and Wales were assessed as being 'good' in a recent round of HMIC inspections when it comes to investigating crime. None were graded as outstanding. Yes, that's right. most British police forces are no good at investigating crime. Its breath-taking that such a fundamental element of policing seems so elusive to so many police forces. And if you think the DEI agenda isn't at least partly responsible then you would sadly, in my experience, be mistaken. Leadership is at the absolute heart of the catastrophic performance problems effecting UK policing at present. To paraphrase the late intellectual and essayist, Christopher Hitchens, it is starting to become obvious how far the termites have spread and how well they have dined. And the termites within British policing have now burrowed so deeply that the rot is really starting to show. The only underrepresented group within policing nowadays it would appear are those who are remotely competent. When I visited underperforming forces (of which there were many) as part of my last role in policing as performance improvement lead at the College of Policing, on many occasions I found deficiencies in leadership, especially at the chief officer level. It became depressingly obvious to me as I travelled around the country that many chief officers I encountered appeared to be completely out of their depth when it came to restoring failing forces, apparently fundamentally lacking the proper operational policing experience to help them do so. They simply could not relate how decisions they were making in their comfortable offices would in any way translate into effective operational policing strategies. I could immediately spot those, admittedly far smaller in number, who were able to get this right, and not surprisingly, these individuals always possessed a solid operational policing pedigree. In other words, they had served their apprenticeship and learnt their trade.

The foregoing may read to some as being an expression of a personal hang up or gripe, but it isn't. I was fortunate enough despite this perverse climate to have progressed in my career up to t/chief superintendent rank. This took hard work, determination, and an element of gritting my teeth and biting my tongue in equal measures. I know that I was fortunate being a white middle-aged man in this emerging DEI arena to progress as far as I did in the service. Like many, I have experienced more than my fair share of professional setbacks, and have been subject to a few stitch ups in promotion processes along the way, normally where another candidate has leapfrogged me for a job, many with less experience or suitability but who in cosmetic terms at least made for better appointments. You have a choice in this scenario; lay down and accept it or continue to struggle on. I chose the latter, but I have seen many colleagues simply give up as they didn't have the stomach for it, the sense of injustice being too much for them. And I completely understand that. Nowadays everyone is assigned a victim group, and, within this victim hierarchy, there are police support organisations standing ready and willing to fight the good fight on behalf of their poor oppressed members. The Association of Women in Policing, Black Police Association, Muslim Police Association, LGBT+ support organisations and on and on it goes. Police force internal intranet pages are crammed full of the information on these groups as they so evidently jostle for position. Every month there seems to be something or other dedicated to one of the victim groups, international women in policing day, international transgender awareness day, transgender Remembrance Day, black history month, and so on and so forth. PRIDE rainbow decals are attached to police vehicles, police officers in uniform 'march' at the various annual LGBT PRIDE events, dancing and marching in full uniform. And all the while, police performance continues to decline, public confidence is shattered, and scandal after scandal continues to rock the reputation of the British police service.

Such an overt and enthusiastic involvement with identity politics not only provides a huge distraction from the core mission of policing, but in ascribing to this political dogma, it divides people into oppressed victim groups rather than seeing people as they are on an individual level. And this, is not diversity, nor is it equality or inclusion. The concept of diversity is far broader than these groups represent it to be, and to quote that arch villain of the left, Dr Jordan Peterson, 'there is more differences within groups than there is between them'. In other words, your assigned victim group does not in any way properly define who you are at an individual level, rather it ascribes the characteristics of that entire group to you, at least in terms of their victim status. This is surely the very definition of racism. And there is nothing very liberal about the concept really. Liberalism in fact believes in the absolute agency of the individual, not the need to ascribe to certain groups based on sex, gender identity, religion, skin colour, or other 'protected' groups.

And this obsession by many senior police officers, civil servants, and politicians, is far from 'inclusive'. As a white middle-aged man, I did not feel remotely included during the latter stages of my own police career. Where was the support organisation for me? Why wasn't I given a victim badge? I'm sure I could have come up with something if asked. I say this tongue in cheek of course. Rather, I found myself walking on eggshells most of the time wondering whether my terminology was up to date and concerned that I might unwittingly offend someone from one of the downtrodden oppressed groups. I can after all, as those who know me will agree, be quite straightforward in my approach and language at times. Once during a Microsoft Teams meeting with colleagues while seconded to the College of Policing (more on that strange experience later!), I was discussing some work with a police force I was engaged with in respect of hard to reach communities. I went on to describe these as 'BAME' communities, the commonly understood term for black and minority ethnic individuals. To my surprise, I was interrupted from my flow and given a sharp rebuke by a junior College of Policing colleague who stated that I was to no longer use that terminology (BAME) as it was now considered 'offensive' and that new terminology had replaced it. This shocked me and admittedly also somewhat pissed me off. The whole thing struck me as disturbingly Orwellian. Perhaps unwisely, I said as much in the meeting, describing this as being akin to Orwell's 'newspeak' from his novel, 1984, whereby one expression had been arbitrarily replaced with another. I tried to convey this observation in a somewhat humorous way, but naturally no one dared find my comment funny.

I don't remember precisely when I became aware of the term 'woke' being used in day to day common language. While no singularly agreed definition of the term exists, the original meaning of woke, as I understand it at least, was a somewhat common-sense and laudable one. In essence, it means to be aware of social and political issues, especially racism. Fine. But that is not how the term is generally interpreted nowadays. It is now more associated with the practice of virtue signalling and false empathy; it is the adherence to a form of cultural Marxism, where identity politics reign supreme. It is the ascribing to the leftist concepts of critical race theory and intersectionality, that there are in society always oppressed groups and oppressor groups. And it is wildly intolerant of contrary narratives and near allergic to any form of debate or discussion that challenges its orthodoxies. It is black and white low-resolution thinking where one group wears halos and the other horns. Woke is in many ways the all encapsulating term for this set of incredibly divisive ideologies. For policing, the indulgence in woke presented as allowing for the infiltration of identity politics, essentially making its presence felt through the establishment of the multitude of internal support groups. However, it wasn't long before this focus shifted more to a public facing display of virtue signalling activity. I think I'm right in saying that the engagement in LGBT PRIDE events was the first time we saw police officers overtly becoming involved in social justice causes. It was certainly my first experience of it. Now, I'm not saying that at one point in history – and that time is thankfully long in the past – that campaigning for gay rights was not an important and necessary cause. The decriminalisation of anti-gay laws was a progressive and necessary step in our society. However, one question I often pondered was whether the police should be overtly involving itself in supporting these PRIDE events, by which I mean marching in full uniform, often while on duty through the streets, some officers even dancing around with fellow participants, appending rainbow coloured PRIDE badges to police vehicles and premises? One school of thought, although not one I have ever ascribed to given there is not one shred of evidence in support of the premise, is that such behaviour shows the police are in touch with wider 'social issues' and by participating in PRIDE events demonstrates that even the police have a sound social conscience. Another school of thought, the one I have always personally maintained, is that regardless of the social cause in question whether gay rights or otherwise, policing should remain neutral and impartial in respect of such causes.

And where does this eager display of identity political virtue signal stop? Can the police service really be all things to all people, especially when so many other groups vie for attention by pinning on the victim badges of oppression? Well, they have certainly tried, albeit have been very selective in which campaigns and political causes they choose to support. When George Floyd was murdered at the hands of a white police officer in 2020 in

Minneapolis, USA, many UK based activists rapidly took to the streets in protest and to call for an end to unarmed black people being killed by white police officers purporting it to be some kind of wild and out of control epidemic. Never mind the fact that a relatively small number of unarmed black people are in fact killed in this way (around 10 instances in the entire USA in 2010), and that by some margin, many more police officers are murdered in the execution of their duty by black males. Indeed, the biggest threat to the lives of black males is in fact other black males. An unpopular statistic in many circles, but one always worth stating I believe. Facts like these simply get in the way of a good protest, and before long, the streets of London were subjected to the disruption caused by largescale Black Lives Matter (BLM) protests which on occasions saw violence directed towards the police. To my utter horror, we soon witnessed Metropolitan Police officers 'taking the knee' in front of baying crowds of predominantly black males in an apparent show of solidarity. From my perspective, this in fact symbolised a complete demonstration of police submission to a baying mob. Watching this open-mouthed at home on TV I could barely believe my eyes. Not only were police officers putting themselves at extreme physical risk by kneeling in front of BLM protestors, but in doing so they were actively taking part in a political demonstration. They had crossed the line. And despite what some might say, BLM is a political cause, being funded mainly in the USA by Democrat Party funders. Yes, it purports to be anti-racist in its mission, but one need only look at its often non-peaceful tactics to see that it is a highly militant and often violent organisation, one who holds the police in particular with a huge amount of disdain and contempt, seeing them as a legitimate enemy. In 2018, the British Transport Police (BTP) announced that it would no longer allow its police vehicles to display poppy decals leading up to Remembrance Day commemoration events in November. The force had allowed this practice for many years previously but were now apparently for some unknown reason bringing it to a close. When challenged on their decision, a senior BTP officer stated that the force had made the decision as they did not want to show support for one charity over another. This was coincidentally around the same time several woke activists were calling for an outright ban on poppies as they considered them to 'glorify war'. Interestingly, BTP continued to allow the display of the LGBT rainbow flag decals on its police vehicles all year round, seemingly having no problems promoting this cause over the nation's fallen servicemen. Fast forward to November 2023 when police were warning against the open display of medals by service men and women travelling into central London to take part in Remembrance Day commemorations. This was due to the risk of the 'offence' this might cause to the huge number of Pro-Palestine protestors who were also taking to the streets of the capital at the same time. So, rather than robustly protect the rights of those who chose to wear poppies or ex-servicemen to wear their medals in honour of our fallen dead, the advice was to take care when displaying them so as to cause no offence to the other, more troublesome group.

In terms of the BLM movement, the taking of the knee syndrome started to take hold following the initial protests in London and elsewhere, and we saw police officers throughout the country gleefully posting photographs on Twitter and other social media platforms of them taking the knee in support of the BLM cause. We had got to a point in UK policing whereby this sort of virtue signalling was not only taken for granted but was being encouraged by many in the police leadership hierarchy. I heard one chief superintendent state that being 'woke' should be a necessary quality of any police leader, and that we should be professing our wokeness from the rooftops whenever we could. And he was not joking! So we now had a situation where many senior leaders within the service, themselves a product of this obsession with DEI and the indulgence in identity politics and virtue signalling, were now those setting the direction and were actively encouraging such behaviour among the rank and file. Those who did not agree, me included, were quietly (at least to begin with) dismissed as simply not being 'on message', of holding to traditional rather than 'progressive' values and ideals. Others, particularly as time went on, were out and out accused of being closet racists, homophobes, or misogynists for not fully embracing this new 'message'. As a chief inspector, I was once asked by my boss why I had never marched at a PRIDE event. I simply stated that I did not believe this to be an effective use of my time or of taxpayer's money. I received some raised eyebrows for simply stating that view, and the sub-text was fully understood; move with the times Dave because it doesn't look good. But the public are no fools, and soon the negative views on this overt police wokery began to appear on social media and elsewhere. The public had seen what was starting to happen, and they weren't happy. Why were police officers in full uniform able to prance around at PRIDE events when crime rates were so high and detections so low? Could police officers seriously justify such acts of collective self-indulgence while response times were so poor and public confidence in the police service so rapidly going down the plughole? Why were police officers getting down on one knee with their heads bowed when they were supposed to be policing activists at a BLM demonstration? Such behaviour was evidently not what most of the public expected of its supposedly politically neutral police service.

Non-Crime Hate Incidents: Policing Hurt Feelings

In 2005, the College of Policing, essentially an expensive quango organisation which reports to the Home Office and exists to supposedly regulate policing standards across the UK, introduced the concept of non-crime hate incidents (NCHI). This was in the wake of the Macpherson report into the murder of black teenager, Stephen Lawrence in London in 1993, and was among several recommendations the inquiry had made. NCHI were designed to deal with incidents, including those relating to comments placed on social media platforms, which were considered to cause offence to anyone who possessed a protected characteristic as defined by the Equality Act. Essentially, this practice which was mandated by the College of Policing for use by all police forces meant that even where no criminal threshold had been reached or criminal offence identified, an individual who had allegedly caused such offence could be reported to the police and would conceivably end up with some form of formal record on police systems for their behaviour which would be classified as a 'hate incident'. In effect, the police in the UK had now began to police the use of speech and offence causing. And unlike the test applied to the establishment of criminal guilt where the threshold for even asserting that an offence has been committed is high and subject to rigid crime recording standards, such non-crime hate incidents were purely perception based. In other words, anyone could freely report such matters to the police, whether the reporter was the intended target of the offence-causing comment or behaviour or not. The stance for the police was therefore in all cases to take the word of the reporter, whether a third party or otherwise, that their feelings had been hurt or offence had been caused and thus the threshold was met for the progression of a NCHI. Under this College of Policing guidance, essentially, anyone could report you for pretty much any perceived offence-causing remark, relatively safe in the knowledge that the police would act. And act they did. No less than 120,000 non-crime hate incidents were recorded by police forces in England and Wales between 2014 and 2019. And if you had been identified as a perpetrator of such NCHI, and a potential future employer requested an enhanced Disclosure Barring Service (DBS) check, the police reserved the right to advise them of your 'hater' status.

Again, many of us within policing expressed more than a sentiment of disquiet and unease about this centrally mandated practice. After all, was it really for the already overburdened and overstretched police service to be responding to what in most cases amounted to instances of hurt feelings? The more commonplace examples included trans people apparently being 'misgendered', certain religious groups believing that their faith had been insulted, or LGBT people taking offence for perceived hurtful comments about their sexuality. Again, I would stress that no criminality had been identified in these instances. More, those identified as the perpetrators would receive a police visit, would be warned about future conduct, asked to 'check their thinking', and their details recorded on police systems as being a recipient of a non-crime hate incident warning. This practice continued for many years, before eventually greater public awareness and political attention was drawn to the practice by the publicity surrounding several high-profile cases and one monumental and significant legal victory. In August 2020, barrister Sarah Phillimore posted on Twitter: "my cat really loves Dreamies perhaps he's a Methodist." For those who don't know, Dreamies are a popular cat treat. Rather provocatively, and indeed suspected to in fact even be testing out the police response to the post, another tweeter reported Phillimore's tweet to local police in South Yorkshire, claiming that her post had caused offence and that it displayed 'anti-Methodist hatred'. According to the complainer, Phillimore had effectively stereotyped all Methodists as "wandering pests that defecate in other people's gardens". You can absolutely see how such an offence-causing conclusion was reached at by the reporter! Whilst many of us would shrug off such nonsense, South Yorkshire Police, sticking rigidly to the College of Policing guidance, determined that Phillimore's comments had indeed met the criteria for a non-crime hate incident for this single tweet and she was dealt with accordingly.

However, the biggest blow to this chilling recording practice occurred on the morning of 21st December 2021 when the Court of Appeal in London ruled that the College of Policing's non-crime hate guidance unlawfully contravenes the right to free expression. The legal challenge was brought by former policeman and Lincolnshire businessman, Harry Miller. Miller was visited by Humberside Police in January 2019 and told that his twitter posts in respect of the transgender debate had been reported and were being treated as a non-crime hate incident. He was duly warned and like many others asked to check his thinking. But rather than simply submit as many before him had done to what amounts to a moral finger wagging, Miller challenged Humberside Police's approach through the courts by way of a number of legal actions which seen his case conclude with a landmark victory.

The Court of Appeal's judgement essentially concluded that the College of Policing mandated enforcement of NCHI's had a "chilling effect" on freedom of speech and that the guidance allowed for virtually any offence-taking to be officially recorded, even the more obviously ridiculous examples such as the Methodist Cat tweet.

Whilst the Court of Appeal did not go as far to instruct the College of Policing to cease the practice, Miller's victory was significant and caused the College to revise it's recording practices relating to reports of NCHI. However, the policing of offence-taking remarks and hurt feeling did not stop as the following cases would go on to demonstrate.

The Lesbian Nana Case

In August 2023, a 16-year-old autistic girl was arrested by seven West Yorkshire police officers for referring to one of them as being a 'lesbian like nana'. The girl and her sister had been attending the Leeds Gay Pride event when the incident occurred. She was arrested by force from her home having been originally conveyed there by police for committing a 'homophobic public order offence'. Yes, for simply making this observation about the officer, a 16-year-old neurodivergent child was forcibly arrested, spent 20 hours in police custody, and was eventually released on bail. The girls mother later complained to the force and all charges were dropped. The incident at time of writing was subject to an investigation by West Yorkshire Police Professional Standards Department. Notwithstanding the absurdity of the entire situation, anyone who knows even a little about autism will understand that they often have an inability to filter what they think before they say it. In this case, the girl simply stated her observation, which was the sole cause for her arrest. And as an aside, the girl's nana is indeed apparently a gay woman which to me removes any *mens rea* (wicked intent) or malice in the comment completely. But even had there been a malicious element to the comment made by a 16-year-old child to an adult female police officer, would the average member of the public expect such an over the top reaction in response? This however is now the low-hanging fruit for some police officers, often spurred on by those in senior positions. Like the NCHI debacle, it is easier to lock people up for causing offence (or in this case more accurately for the officer taking offence) than it is pursuing those in society who cause the real harm such as serious and organised criminals involved in drugs supply, or those who commit crime affecting many neighbourhoods such as robbery, burglary, or car crime. Dealing with these more serious crimes takes actual police work and the necessary investigative and detection skills, something which many police leaders are themselves lacking in. So, in some instances, encouraging others to grab at the low hanging fruit is preferable.

The Wakefield Koran Case

In February 2023, again in the West Yorkshire region, this time Wakefield, another child with autism, a 14-year old boy was forced to flee his home with his mother and go into hiding, fearing for his life. His crime? Bringing a copy of the Koran to school and accidentally damaging it. The boy in question had lost a bet with his friends, the forfeit being that he must purchase a copy of the Koran and bring it to school. Whilst admittedly a foolhardy and perhaps risky endeavour, particularly given the religious value placed on the book by Muslims, in no way could we have predicted what followed an otherwise innocuous incident of the Koran in question getting slightly scuffed when it was dropped in the school playground.

In response, the school immediately suspended the boy and three fellow pupils and the matter was reported to West Yorkshire Police who, yes, you guessed it, began with haste and ruthless efficiency to record and investigate the matter as a 'hate incident'. Furthermore, a local Muslim Labour councillor for reasons unknown decided to embellish the scenario and communicated on social media that the Koran had in fact been desecrated (it had not been) thus creating further tension and interest. He stated in one now deleted twitter post that 'serious provocative action' needed to be dealt with urgently by the police, the school, and the local authority.

The boys mother received many threats from members of the local Muslim community including death threats and threats of arson directed at her home and family. She was forced to vacate her home and effectively go into hiding rightly taking the threats that had been made extremely seriously. And who could blame her. Radical Islam has a track record of backing up such threats with force and have done so innumerable times in response to any perceived desecration of the religion or the insulting of their prophet. But rather than take such threats seriously themselves, instead West Yorkshire Police decided that a better course of action would be to facilitate a press conference where the local Imam, Councillor, head teacher and the boy's mother were present along with local West Yorkshire Police Chief Inspector Andy Thornton. At this meeting the Koran in question was publicly inspected by the Imam to assert whether in his view it had indeed been desecrated. To his credit, the Imam did call for calm among the local Muslim Community. Nothing was mentioned about the death threats. A few days later, the boy's mother attended a further meeting, this time at the local mosque after Friday prayers where, in front of an all-male group, and accompanied by the school's head teacher, Mr Griffiths, she pled for the forgiveness of her son. She told of the death threats she and her son had received and the impact it had had on her family and made an unreserved apology, asking that they now be left alone. Griffiths also delivered a grovelling apology to the assembled males expressing his 'sorrow' that the situation had occurred and thanking the mosque for providing them with an audience.

And this all happened, not in some middle eastern country governed by Sharia Law, but in the United Kingdom! One shudders to contemplate what would have happened if, at the first meeting, the Imam had proclaimed desecration of the holy book, or had the child's mother decided to ignore the threats and accept the risk. It's not worth thinking about. But this situation shows how quickly West Yorkshire Police were to investigate and record the matter as a non-crime hate incident and were then firmly at the centre of the circus that ensued. Rather than focus on the death threats that the boy and his mother had received, threats that caused them to flee their home, their entire strategy was that of placating the local Muslim community and soothing their hurt feelings. When you step back from this situation, such behaviour under the guiding hand of a West Yorkshire Police chief inspector surely cannot be considered as rational or acceptable. And perhaps of no great surprise, no person was ever identified or charged in connection with the death threats issued.

These incidents do not amount to isolated 'one-off' occurrences. Let's not forget the stark figure of 120,000 non-crime hate incidents recorded and investigated by police over a five-year period. Responding to these types of incidents became the bread and butter work of our police and seemed preferable to undertaking the proper crime fighting that had undisputedly been the core mission when I joined the service. Nor had this happened without the necessary socio-political influences, many of which we have already discussed. But somewhere along the line, the British police lost its sense of its core mission and with it, the concept of neutrality, of being truly independent of politics in every sense of the term. The liberal left ideologies of identity politics, intersectionality, and critical race theory had firmly taken hold within the British policing establishment. And chief police officers, rather than resist the pernicious effects such influences were beginning to have within policing, warmly embraced the practices, many themselves having been beneficiaries of the DEI equity agenda.

By the second decade of the twenty-first century, British Policing was taking an unrecognisable form. The obsession with expressing its ever-sharpened social conscience had become all consuming, especially for those at the top of the service, and the dirty job of policing for many had become something of a lesser priority. Unless a protected victim group was being discussed, the priorities of conventional crime fighting began to take a back seat to the social justice pandering both internally and externally, the transition to the latter being a natural progression as the former became more embedded in police decision-making strategy and structures.

Those such as I with traditional values were being dismissed as being 'out of touch' or 'old fashioned'. Every interview or promotion board process was now crammed full of DEI related questions, replacing the need for the candidate to convey evidence of technical competency. Instead, the 'softer skills' were now in demand taking precedence over actual police competency. And so, the slippery slope had not only begun, but was in total free-fall to oblivion. Police forces were underperforming at an alarming rate in respect of traditional crime performance measures such as reductions in crime and increases in arrests and detections and more forces than at any time in history were being placed into 'special measures' by the police inspectorate under the tenure of the then Home Secretary, Suella Braverman. Braverman had taken a correctly robust stance against police 'wokery'; she called the police out on their involvement in identity politics which she considered inappropriate for a supposedly neutral police service, along with the numerous displays of wasteful virtue signalling activity that went with it. Braverman held up a mirror to British police chiefs and many did not like what they saw. The Home Secretary introduced performance targets, put pressure on the police inspectorate to name and shame underperforming forces and began to intrude on operational priorities that she felt chief constables needed to be addressing. These were specifically not to be the indulgence in woke identity politics, but to begin to restore public trust by getting on with the actual job of policing. The National Police Chiefs Council, the organisation which represents all officers and civilian equivalent of Assistant Chief Constable or above, openly criticised Braverman for crossing the line of constabulary independence. But the question instead should have been why did a home secretary feel the need to do so in the first place? The Home Secretary fully understood the convention of operational independence, a jealously guarded concept by the chief constables and their Metropolitan Police equivalents when it suits their agenda, but she decided to speak out regardless. The truth of the matter was that Braverman had well and truly sensed the mood music that the public were growing tired of an ineffective police service and so decided to directly intervene. She called for more proactivity, more stop and searches to be conducted in an effort to reduce violent crime and knife carrying, and mandated that police forces should personally attend crimes such as burglary, all designed to restore public trust and re-set policing back to its core mission. She also specifically instructed the police service not to indulge in identity political causes, but to ensure a greater degree of neutrality. For those at the top of the service, it seemed that the game might be up, and that for once in many of their careers, they would be expected to lead proper police operations rather than painting their faces in rainbow colours and only taking to the streets during Pride events. I was beginning to feel optimistic.

CHAPTER 4

End of the policing mission: What are the Police For?

Regrettably, Home Secretary's come and go, and so was the case with Suella Braverman who resigned under extreme pressure in late 2023 for speaking out too many times against poor policing practices. She was of course totally correct to do so, but she lacked the crucial support of the Prime Minister and was sent on her way. Her last (and largely accurate) observation was the two-tier policing used by the Met when it came to managing protest and large-scale public order events. Braverman said that it was clear that the Met adopted a far softer response when dealing with left-wing activists than with those from the opposing end of the political spectrum. As a former gold (strategic) public order commander I can certainly attest that public order policing is a complex business, particularly when it comes to political protest. Nevertheless, Braverman was certainly on to something and the Met hierarchy knew it. A collective sigh of relief could therefore be heard from many parts of government, civil servants, and chief police officers when Braverman left office. The College of Policing who had been in Braverman's crosshairs since she took office, and who she had specifically identified as being at least partly responsible for promoting the woke agenda into policing, was for now seemingly off the hook. The outspoken Home Secretary had been silenced and the emperors could once again go around comfortably naked.

One other issue Braverman had highlighted, and one I had personally expressed my concern about for many years, was the fact that more and more non-policing demand had now fallen to the police service. Mental health and other 'vulnerability' demand had in particular already caused a huge strain on every police force in the land, a situation that the police have seemingly slept walked into over the last decade or so with little or no challenge to the additional demand being placed on the service by those in charge. The Metropolitan Police Service announced in 2023 (coincidentally just after being placed into Special Measures by the policing inspectorate) that they would no longer attend mental health related calls. This seemed to cause a somewhat polarising response amongst media and other commentators. I was surprised just how critical some were about this decision; particularly as a handful of other forces had already taken this approach under the Right Care Right Person scheme well before the Met's announcement.

Before getting into the rights and wrongs of this particular decision, it did occur to me that this was yet another example of how apparently 'schizophrenic' our media has become in its reporting of police related stories, especially those emanating from the Met. The Commissioner had rightly been charged with addressing the increased levels of violent crime in the capital, particularly crime involving youth homicide and knife carrying. However, when he proactively invoked measures such as this to put his front-line officers to better use by reducing time spent on what is essentially non-police demand, he is criticised for doing so. It seemed that Sir Mark Rowley couldn't do right for doing wrong!

I had been advocating a similar approach to that taken by the Met for a long while. I remember as a divisional operations superintendent, I became increasingly frustrated when reading the overnight incident logs at just how much of my officer's time was spent dealing with these issues. The standard mental health call would go something like this: A call for service would come into the police control room from a member of the public reporting someone suffering from some sort of mental health crisis in a public place. The officers would be duly dispatched normally on an immediate grade attendance (normally they wouldn't even try to source an ambulance as they rarely attend such calls) and the police officers would invariably end up detaining the individual under the mental health act, taking them to a hospital accident and emergency department, and waiting for anything up to eight hours until the person could be assessed by a psychiatrist, generally deemed fit thereafter to be released from care. Go to any A&E department any day of the week, and you'll see just as many police vehicles parked up outside as you will ambulances. This is the reason.

You see, unlike dealing with the normal clientele who require police detention and arrest powers, the police generally have no access to information needed to properly inform decision making in respect of mental health matters. So, whilst a police officer can check the Police National Computer, Intelligence Databases and so on to help inform whether an individual needs to be arrested, or can be dealt with in another manner, as well as assessing the risks and past behaviours of that individual, police officers have no such access to a person's mental health profile. What this has led to is an ingrained risk averse mindset whereby the default approach is to err on the side of caution, detaining the individual under the mental health act, and letting others with access to information about the individual (most are already known to NHS psychiatric services) along with a far better level of professional training, to make the decisions about the correct level of response. This may not always be mental health detention, and other solutions will be available depending on the individuals existing diagnosis and treatment plan. The downside of course is that police officers effectively become an expensive taxi service to hospital A&E departments or other receiving centres, hardly an effective use of police resources.

Now, some forces have to their credit tried to be innovative over the years in addressing these issues. This has included pairing police officers with psychiatric nurses in police patrol cars to respond to such calls, embedding mental health practitioners in police control rooms who can support decision-making, and some health boards have established out of hours triage services to help advice and support police officers responding to such calls. But such initiatives simply serve to mask the overall problem which is that police officers simply should not routinely be the first line of response to attend to this sort of societal issue.

I can hear some say, if not the police then who? I could be glib and suggest that this isn't a problem for the police to solve. Surely the financially bloated NHS could, and should, service this demand. After all, mental health is as the terms suggests, a health issue and not a law enforcement problem. You could ask an electrician to come out and fix a burst pipe at your house. The electrician would probably be ill-equipped, unqualified, and most likely too busy trying to sort out electrical things rather than plumbing problems. But maybe he'll turn up and do his best if there are not enough plumbers around to help. And this is exactly where we have ended up with mental health matters in the UK. Police officers are trained in law-enforcement, in the criminal law, and in essentially how to prevent and detect crime. Some would contest this characterisation as being too simplistic and by claiming that policing is so much more than merely crime prevention and detection, and I would possibly agree. But that 'so much more' should surely not extend beyond the occupational discipline and competency of policing by in effect straying into the territory of other professions. Would you want a police officer appearing at your child's school to deliver a maths lesson because there was a shortage of maths teachers? Of course not.

And mental health demand is not insignificant in nature; in 2022 it was estimated that police officers spent between 20% and 40% of their time dealing with mental health related incidents. It cannot be any coincidence then that whilst police officers have sleepwalked into assuming this responsibility over the last decade or so, policing has begun to drift from its conventional neighbourhood policing activity and proactive anti-crime operations as it has veered into this mental health response guardian mode. Yes, there have been other challenges including massive funding blows delivered by Cameron and May's Tory administration, but surely that should have been all the more reason to strip out those non-core functions such as mental health response and concentrate on conventional law enforcement activity. But that is not what happened, instead policing steadily assumed responsibility for this demand, often applying sticking plasters every so often to make it easier to manage. At a strategic level within policing, there was a collective burying of heads in the sand, hoping it would eventually go away and that servicing this non-crime demand wouldn't impact on conventional performance too much. All the while, frontline officers were being exposed to a new level of risk, one they had little training for.

Some within policing even capitalised on this new 'specialism', as many forces reacted (or knee jerked) by establishing mental health and suicide prevention hubs to deal with the increase in mental health demand and the growing expectations on how the police were expected to respond, including the constant administrative cycle of referrals to partner agencies; it's not simply the immediate response demand that has applied pressure to policing, it has impacted back office functions just as much. Mental health soon became a substantial policing enterprise, but one rarely discussed in crime performance settings or acknowledged by senior leaders as a cause and effect for steady reductions in crime detection rates and public confidence. And all the while, frontline police officers were slowly but surely becoming more and more de-skilled in conventional crime prevention and detection techniques given the less time they spent on such activity and how much of their time was being taken up by mental health calls. More reported crimes are now being 'screened out' whereby no physical police attendance will take place, desk top investigation teams have been created, less and less incidents are receiving a physical police attendance, and even significant crimes such as domestic burglary reports are now no longer meeting the attendance threshold in the same way as a call for someone suffering from mental health crisis. Post 2010, policing had significantly fewer frontline officers with increasing levels of non-crime related mental health demand. So, inevitably something was always going to give.

It's of little surprise therefore that there has been no 'winners' in this scenario. Aside from the obvious knock on impact on police activity in more conventional areas, communities have experienced less visible policing, responsiveness has been poor in respect of other calls for service, and new officers entering the service now have far less exposure to bread and butter police functions which, as a symptom, is now beginning to clearly show out in HMICFRS inspections as more and more forces are found to be failing on policing basics including the investigation of crime. However, critically, this arrangement does not in any way properly serve those who suffer from mental health crisis. Police officers are not properly trained or equipped to deal with complex mental health problems, and the default method of mental health detention does not provide a sustainable solution nor does it offer the correct level of care to those who most need it. It is an unfair risk to place on an already overburdened police service.

I welcome the decision taken by the Met and a handful of other forces to transfer responsibility of this demand to those better placed to respond to it. The problem however remains that the police service has unwittingly now assumed responsibility for mental health incidents which has become such an ingrained part of frontline policing demand. It will take high level buy-in and a consistent strategic approach to disentangle it. Whilst some NHS trusts and Ambulance Services may well be receptive to assuming this responsibility, many will not. Despite forces receiving detailed legal advice on the matter, I suspect that there may well be counter challenges from the prospective receiving agencies who will, understandably, be reluctant to assume this high volume and complex demand.

Whatever strategic approach is taken by policing and its partners to tackle this issue; the starting assumption must be an acceptance that response to such matters will no longer routinely fall to the police. Of course, there will continue to be calls where mental health and criminality intersect, and those incidents will remain, at least in respect of initial attendance a matter for the police. However, for those that from the outset present to police control rooms as being purely a mental health matter with no criminality or violence involved, there must be an acceptance that the police will not respond to such matters, instead passing to the relevant local partners whether the ambulance service or other agency. If increased capacity and investment is required in respect of NHS and mental health providers then so be it, and rightly policing should afford a sensible period of transition to handover such arrangements to the partner best placed to deliver the service. Green shoots are appearing in forces such as Humberside Police who have worked tirelessly with its local NHS and Ambulance Service partners to put such arrangements in place. This has not been easy or straightforward and it is a testament to the force executive and its local partners for reaching such agreements. Incidentally, Humberside is now one of the best performing police forces in England and Wales. It is understandable that other forces are now looking to the Humberside model and its 'Right Care Right Person' scheme as being promising practice. The challenge will be taking local partners with them on the journey.

CHAPTER 5

Politics and Police Leadership: One step forward for politics, two steps back for leadership

Policing has always been something of a hot topic in political terms, and arguably has also been subject to more political reform than any other public sector organisation, particularly in respect of its structures of accountability. Prior to the Police Act of 1964 there were two broad systems of governance of the police outside London (the City of London and the Metropolitan Police have always been treated differently). In urban areas there were Watch Committees, comprised wholly of local councillors who were often very active in their oversight of their forces. In rural areas there were Joint Standing Committees which were dominated by local (and non-elected) magistrates and arguably exercised less day-to-day control over the chief officers of their local force.

The 1964 Act Created the same system for all police forces outside London. The tripartite system of accountability was introduced whereby there were now three elements: The Home Secretary, the Chief Constable, and the local police authority. The important aspect of the 1964 Act was that Chief Constables were given direction and control of their forces so that local authorities had less operational influence than they once had. This element of direction and control has since come to be known as operational independence or constabulary independence. Essentially, setting this aspect out in statute sought to insulate chief constables from political interference in policing matters from any other player in the tripartite structure. The tripartite triangle was perhaps not equal, it was skewed towards the Chief Constable and the Home Secretary. The City of London Police continued to be responsible to the City of London Authority and the Metropolitan Police to the Home Secretary, now a joint accountability arrangement involving the London Mayor and Home Secretary.

Various statutory reforms followed the seminal 1964 Act including the Police and Criminal Evidence Act 1984, Police and Magistrates Court Act 1994, Crime and Disorder Act 1998, Police Reform Act 2002, and Police Reform and Social Responsibility Act 2011. Each of these legislative changes brought about some alteration to police accountability structures, some more significant than others. Centralised performance targets were introduced, an independent police complaints body was established, the composition of police authority membership was changed, and arguably most significantly, the 2011 Police Reform Act swept away Police Authorities and replaced them with directly elected local Police and Crime Commissioners. Turnout for such PCC elections have always been low, with the latest PCC UK-wide elections held in May 2021 attracting only 33% of eligible voters.

On doing away with the tripartite structure and police authorities, the government effectively put the public in charge of who would be responsible for crime and policing in their force area and ultimately who would hold the local chief constable to account. The remit of the PCC is vast. They have the responsibility along with the Chief Constable to set the police and crime plan which establishes the crime priorities of the force, are responsible for hiring and if needs be firing the chief constable, and set the council tax precept budget for policing. However, most controversially, well certainly for those in policing, is that some PCC's get perhaps a little too involved in operational policing matters, often tiptoeing over the line that is constabulary independence. The biggest challenge however is that the term 'operational independence' or 'constabulary independence' has never been defined anywhere in statute. A decision made by the High Court in 2017 did not help to fully clarify matters either, albeit it suggested that PCC's do indeed have a remit which extends to operational policing matters. In this case, the then Chief Constable of South Yorkshire Police, David Crompton, sought a judicial review of the actions taken by the force's PCC,

Alan Billings in respect of a number of matters, not least of which was to suspend him. However, most relevant here is that the High Court in respect of operational independence found the following:

1. It is right to observe... that the operational independence of the Chief Constable is repeatedly recognised in the Policing Protocol. However, the PCC is obliged to hold the Chief Constable to account for every function he performs. In our judgment, matters relevant to operational independence are not excluded from the scope of the PCC's powers of scrutiny. The operational independence at common law .... must give way, if so required, by the terms of the 2011 Act and, in our judgment, the Act qualifies that common law rule.

2. The Act adopts a more nuanced approach than the common law in this regard, recognising in the Protocol it introduces both the importance of operational independence and an important competing imperative, namely democratic oversight of the police. It is, in our judgment, impossible to see operational independence as being beyond the supervision of the PCC.

This judgement, while carefully worded, left the door somewhat ajar for PCC's to test this concept further, and only through further court proceedings and their findings will this perhaps be more comprehensively established. Some PCC's have become more involved than others in operational matters, but in limited, more subtle ways, possibly being shrewd enough to recognise the risks that intruding in operational policing issues might create for them. Some have fronted media interviews when discussing operational matters with the Chief Constable neatly shoved into the background. This is somewhat disconcerting as it might well suggest that the power dynamic and thus decision making is similarly reflected behind closed doors. Then there is the political dimension itself. The majority of PCC's are themselves members of a political party (currently 85% of PCC's are active

Conservatives), and many strive for higher office further down the line. It is fair then to say that the political views of whichever party occupies the PCC's seat will inevitably have an impact on local policing priorities. Does this not bring politics a step too close to policing and further risk the concept of constabulary independence? Time, I suppose will tell!

It's Leadership, Stupid

I've met many experienced, capable, and talented chief officers (assistant chief constables and above) over the years. I've also met others who it might euphemistically be said have less of a grasp on the realities of police work. You can spot pretty quickly those who have served their apprenticeship and gained valuable 'boots on the ground' exposure from the latter who have normally been fast-tracked up through the ranks without being exposed to the difficult or dangerous or who are perhaps a product of direct entry schemes. They simply do not (and cannot) understand the variety and complexity of the challenges that day to day operational policing entails or the pressures it places to those on its front line. That isn't a criticism, it's just the reality of how the service now often identifies and selects its senior leaders. Operational competency and experience are much less attractive now than the softer leadership qualities required through the integrated competency framework. It is almost taken for granted that once you reach a certain level in the service you have the necessary operational exposure required to fulfil senior roles; this is an incorrect and sometimes dangerous assumption because it is rarely tested in any senior selection process.

Chief officers perform a critical role in any force, and ultimately set the strategic direction of the organisation, defining its culture and tone, and ideally provide their own leadership through the demonstration of personal values. Crucially, they are ultimately custodians of the concept of 'operational independence' and must stand up to and defend robustly any political interference in professional policing matters. Sadly, we have seen many examples where this line has become increasingly blurred and even outright crossed, and arguably this is because chiefs have allowed this to happen by being too passive or reluctant to challenge. You only have to look at the way politicians have been wading into various policing issues lately, and how many chiefs have remained silent and have not stood up and challenged what is often ill-informed observations and armchair critique of police decision-making to fit a populist political point. It's also concerning to see an increasing amount of PCC's provide press briefings in response to operational matters be they serious crime related or civil emergencies. This is not the function of the PCC and if the matter is so serious to warrant it, a senior police officer should provide the press briefing and will most certainly do so with a greater degree of professional knowledge and credibility. Chief police officers (Assistant chief constable rank and above - the Met and City of London Police have a different chief officer rank structure) perform critical roles in any force. They ultimately shape the strategic direction of the force, define its tone and culture, shape the operational priorities, create, and maintain relationships with strategic stakeholders, and ultimately have responsibility for the quality of service provided to the public. They are the police force's executive team; between them, they run the show and so must stand to account for what goes on and for the key decisions made.

Recognising the criticality of the chief officer role and those within the service who occupy them, and following a review conducted by the college of policing, in June 2023 the strategic command course (SCC) the long standing training program designed to prepare superintendents for chief officer roles within the service was replaced by a new police executive leadership program (PELP). The SCC had consisted of a 3-month residential program at the College of Policing, Ryton, the prelude to which was attending and passing the reputedly rigorous 2-day senior police national assessment centre (SPNAC). However, following a period of fairly rapid consultation with Chief Constables through National Police Chiefs Council in 2023, it was determined that SPNAC and SCC were no longer fit for purpose, a key reason being that it was now felt that SPNAC had become something that candidates were being actively coached to pass, often using private consultants who were normally themselves former College of Policing SPNAC assessors. Whilst this does of course raise some ethical concerns over equality of opportunity to such expensive coaching providers, I couldn't see the issue with coaching as a concept per se as, after all, we regularly coach candidates to pass promotion processes at virtually every other rank, often more intensively for those in underrepresented groups. The other fundamental concern was that SCC had itself lacked 'inclusivity'. It was suggested that it may potentially exclude for example working mothers or those with caring responsibilities in respect of the pressures it placed on being away from home for such an extended period. The other main criticism was the mechanism by which candidates were supported and selected for SCC in that it was wholly depended on chief constables endorsing them, this often being done in an inconsistent and subjective basis, a practice often cited as being less than transparent.

So, what changed with the new process? Well, following broad agreement that SCC needed to be replaced, the question became what exactly it should be replaced with. To start with, and in order to address the inclusivity conundrum, the college of policing determined that a new non-residential module-based system over a period of 12 months was the preferred mechanism, thus achieving greater opportunity and inclusivity for prospective candidates, particularly those who had apparently been put off by the SCC's 3 month residential commitment. The other thing to change was the selection process for entry onto the new executive leadership program which would replace the former two-day assessment centre. The college determined that this was best achieved by means of a competency-based portfolio of evidence submitted by superintendents which would be independently assessed by the College, taking into consideration the comments of the respective Chief Constable. However, to remove the element of subjectivity, inconsistency, and often perceived unfairness, the College would in this instance have the final determination on who would be admitted to the new PELP on assessment of the competency portfolio. This all seemed eminently sensible.

But this is UK policing, and as Robert Burns once famously wrote, the best laid plans of mice and men. So, as the revised selection process began to dawn on chiefs, and with it the realisation that their decision making role in respect of selection to the program had been significantly diminished, a new round of discussions began in which chiefs sought to reinsert themselves more substantially into the selection decision-making loop. This was concerning given that the whole ambition of the new portfolio process was designed to make chiefs sit on their hands. But those hands were becoming increasingly restless, and some chiefs simply needed to have a firmer grip on the decision-making tiller. And so, the biggest blow was delivered to this ambitious new process, and chiefs began to exert influence and re-assert virtually the same autonomy they held under the previous system. The chiefs had in essence removed the role of the college in centrally assessing these portfolio submissions, and instead they would now undertake this function personally, the 'compromise' being that they would be aided in this process by a college of policing advisor. In other words, the very subjectivity that was to be designed out of the process was effectively inserted back into it. Chief constables now once again had an all-powerful role in determining which of their aspiring candidates would be supported, and in effect offered a place on the new PELP process, and which would not.

As I've said, one of the many problems in policing is that the service advances and promotes people in its own image. Promotion and selection criteria goalposts are moved each time a new chief takes up residence and has his or her own perspective on what constitutes a good leader. Some look for a well-rounded operational policing pedigree, along with the desired leadership attributes. I have no problem with that. Others, especially in the current DEI fixated era who are consumed with diversity and inclusion matters will look for evidence of this aspect, in other words how well does the candidate show that they subscribe to the DEI ideology, regardless of their technical policing attributes. The latter example being significantly more desirable in today's world of police promotion. Regardless, it is surely the very definition of subjectivity, something which to their credit the College of Policing were in fact trying to engineer out of chief officer selection processes. A further observation about the new PELP process is that one of its stated aims was to increase the number of 'underrepresented' groups in chief officer roles. The definition of 'underrepresented' in this case was females and candidates who identify as BAME. This very much aligns to the wider ambition of the service to be more representative of its communities. As previously noted, this has always been a tricky issue for the service who have tried various measures to increase representation including targeted recruitment processes and a variety of positive action initiatives to support underrepresented groups through the recruitment and selection processes. Despite these initiatives, little seems to have changed, and many chiefs and PCC's feel under increasing pressure to make greater inroads. The chief constable of West Yorkshire Police recently called for a change in the law to allow for positive discrimination to be permitted to increase levels of BAME representation within his force. Positive discrimination being code here for lowering entry standards, sifting out white male applicants, and allowing less qualified members of the BAME community to join the service. After all, what do standards matter so long as the optics are good.

Part of the PELP portfolio submission process was the requirement on applicants to submit a detailed diversity monitoring form as part of their application. Those who failed to submit this information were advised that their application could not be progressed without it. Given the already opaque selection process that had been decided upon partly as a result of the intervention by chiefs, this did nothing to provide candidates with confidence that diversity information might not in fact be used as part of the overall selection process to ensure the desired increase in representation. One police contact even told me that on inquiring about applying for PELP a chief officer advised him that the process was not really for 'people like him', but was designed to uplift the number of those from underrepresented groups to the chief officer ranks. The aspiring applicant in question being a white middle-aged male. Yes, this is entirely anecdotal, but I have no reason to disbelieve it, particularly given everything else we see happening. It is difficult therefore not to adopt a degree of cynicism in what has become an already fairly bewildering process, and in this regard I hope the College of Policing might well reflect on this aspect for future PELP intakes, even if simply to make the process clearer for candidates (and Chiefs) and to avoid any such perceived negative perceptions and cynicism from those aspiring to apply for the program in the future. Fairness, transparency, and a sense of meritocracy surely must be at the heart of any effective selection process, particularly for those aspiring to the most senior levels of policing. Any suggestion of bias being engineered into the process to increase the selection of underrepresented groups must surely be swiftly refuted, and where necessary evidence provided to address any such concerns. Whilst requesting candidates to supply detailed diversity monitoring information as part of the PELP portfolio submission process will undoubtedly be defended as standard practice, it does leave the door open for unhelpful conclusions to be reached, and surely such processes therefore would be far better designed to be colour and gender blind to ensure the best candidates are being selected for such critical policing roles regardless of any other characteristics?

The College of Policing must however be credited with at least trying to reform the system of chief officer selection, even if it did not completely succeed in its ambitions. Trying to implement such a significant change and in such a short period of time whilst corralling 43 chief constables in the process is never a straightforward task. The decision to centralise decision-making in respect of PELP portfolio applications was the correct one, and it is regrettable that the College acceded to chief constables in this regard. This was counterintuitive to securing national standards on the selection of chief officers, and when you consider that SPNAC had previously fulfilled this role and done so centrally this was in fact a regressive step. This is a fundamental element and securing a process of selection to the PELP independently of chiefs must surely be the gold standard. To be fair, the College are in the process of reforming and setting out new leadership standards for every rank, so there is certainly an ambition on their part to set these standards nationally. After all, it simply cannot be right that an individual can for example undertake a superintendent promotion process in one force, spectacularly fail that process, only to apply to another force, and be successful. And this isn't a hypothetical scenario; it happens. This goes back to the subjectivity concern whereby although chiefs may indeed profess to use the College of Policing competency and values framework in their promotion and selection processes, the evidence would suggest the reality is often quite different. And the same concerns are wholly relevant to the new PELP process. One chief constables' assessment of a portfolio may differ significantly from that of his peer, even with the aid of a cadre of College advisors who, will more than likely, be influenced by the views of the respective chief in any case

To allay any concerns – and concerns do exist – that the new PELP process is a mechanism to simply progress more underrepresented groups to the chief officer ranks, the system should be constructed in a way that anonymises personal characteristics such as sex and race until such a point as a full evaluation of the evidence has been made and a conclusion reached on candidate suitability. Only then should such detailed diversity information be made available to those in any way involved in the selection process. It cannot be denied that the introduction of PELP was a highly ambitious step to reform the system of chief officer selection, and that from the outset a clear set of objectives were present on the part of the College of Policing to make the system more accessible, inclusive and crucially to take chiefs much more out of the decision making loop in respect of a candidates suitability and progression. However, for all the reasons outlined, it has most certainly I submit been a missed opportunity.

CHAPTER 6

Sexists, Racists, and Misogynists

In June 2023 Police Scotland's chief constable, Sir Iain Livingstone, landed a bombshell merely weeks ahead of his planned retirement. At an appearance before the Scottish Police Authority he declared that he had concluded his force to be 'institutionally racist and discriminatory'. While many applauded him for being progressive in taking this stance, the Scottish Police Federation did not react nearly so positively, claiming that Sir Iain's proclamation suggests that the workforce of Police Scotland are themselves racist, sexist, and misogynistic at an individual level. Sir Iain on his subsequent media rounds went out of his way to explain the meaning of institutional racism as he understood it, but by then the genie was well and truly out of the bottle and the term was being spun by media and other pundits in a similar fashion to the post-Macpherson climate.

The Police Scotland Assistant Chief Constable charged with leading on the force diversity, inclusion and equality strategy was interviewed on a Sunday Politics television program and was asked by the presenter about the data used to inform Sir Iain's statement. He did not go on to provide specific facts and figures however, instead using terms such as we've consulted with BAME communities and have listened to the perceptions of individuals in reaching this conclusion. When pressed by the interviewer to provide specific examples of the policies, procedures and practices within the force that were considered institutionally discriminatory, the assistant chief constable spoke about how ill-fitting body armour for female officers likely constitutes internal discrimination. Like me, I'm sure those sitting at home watching this interview were left scratching their heads wondering just what it is that's so bad within this organisation that has led to such a damning statement by the chief constable. From that interview, I for one was certainly no further forward in my understanding of the situation. This is somewhat unhelpful for both Police Scotland's own employees and indeed for the public who were likely trying to get a sense of the current crisis facing their police service.

The data that led to such a conclusion and the resulting significant announcement, thought to be the first of its kind by a UK police chief, may well undoubtedly exist, and I had hoped that it may even be placed into the public domain. Whilst this may have made for uncomfortable reading, it would at the very least help people understand why the chief took this decision. No such data has been forthcoming. Regardless, Police Scotland will face some significant challenges in the weeks and months ahead and, as ever, those on the frontline of policing will feel the impact most severely. I vividly recall being a young constable in the post-Macpherson 1990's, and well remember the public backlash my colleagues and I experienced as we went about an already difficult and at times dangerous and hostile occupation. You were no longer just a 'pig' or 'the filth' but were now in fact seemingly a racist too. Depressingly, 25 years on, my frontline colleagues in Scotland are I suspect set to experience much of this same abuse. Perhaps a price worth paying to achieve longer term reform some might say, but this will be a substantial test of Police Scotland's leadership in supporting its workforce as they navigate through some incredibly choppy waters. Recruitment and retention matters must also be considered.

This leads us to the term 'institutional racism' itself. When Sir William Macpherson used it in the wake of the horrendous murder of Stephen Lawrence, he carefully set out his definition of the term. Institutional racism was defined by Macpherson as: "the collective failure of an organisation to provide an appropriate and professional service to people because of their colour, culture, or ethnic origin. It can be seen or detected in processes, attitudes and behaviour that amount to discrimination through prejudice, ignorance, thoughtlessness, and racist stereotyping which disadvantage minority ethnic people". Since then, the term has been used on several occasions, often with subtle nuances placed on its definition and meaning. No universally agreed definition of 'institutional racism' exist, although Macpherson's I would suggest comes very close to it. It could nonetheless be argued that the term remains somewhat ambiguous in nature, misunderstood, misinterpreted (often on purpose) and has been over politicised. Met Commissioner Sir Mark Rowley himself recently stated as much when explaining his reasons for refusing to accept the label as it relates to his own organisation following the Casey review which followed the tragic murder of Sarah Everard at the hands of a serving Metropolitan police officer.

So, what next for the British police service, once considered to be the finest in the world? How do we go about restoring that proud reputation whilst re-connecting with the public, providing them trust and confidence in their police? In my assessment several things need to be considered; firstly, the 'mission' of policing needs to be re-defined both to the public and internally within police organisations themselves. Over the past decade or so, policing has suffered something of an identity crisis as we have imported more responsibility and demand from other public sector agencies, most notably those responsible for mental health provision. This has led to a huge amount of time being spent by frontline police officers dealing with those suffering mental health crisis and vulnerability demand, and therefore much less time on proactive prevention and detection activity. This has in turn been at least part responsible in the gradual de skilling of officers in respect of what were once core policing functions with more forces than ever being placed by His Majesty's Inspector into 'special measures', and many more being found seriously underperforming in fundamental areas such as public contact and investigation of crime. Policing is, I would suggest, in serious need of a 'factory reset' to help bring it back to its core functions of crime prevention and detection, and this will surely go some way to re-establishing trust and confidence within our communities, providing it is carried out ethically, proportionately, and fairly.

Policing has undoubtedly become more politicised than ever over the last decade or so, with more control and direction being exerted by the 'centre' through the Home Office and as a result much less control being exercised by locally elected Police and Crime Commissioners. This resonates with the tensions experienced in the previous tripartite structure of accountability whereby Police Authorities as the forerunners to PCC's were gradually squeezed of their share of power to the benefit of Chiefs and the Home Office. Such power relationships have never been truly equal, and PCC's are now experiencing the same tensions with more 'top down' direction coming from ministers whereby effectively the national policing priorities now trump the local. Admittedly, some of this home Office intrusion has been necessary as it becomes more evident that policing is beginning to fall apart at the seams.

Police and crime related 'stories' have always attracted media attention, whether relating to crime, disorder or other local crime issues. The gorier the better, or to quote a journalistic phrase, 'if it bleeds, it leads'! More recently however, this focus has shifted more to the internal organisational issues impacting the police service such as misconduct, vetting, and criminality by serving officers. The 'one or two bad apples in the barrel' analogy is now no longer a convincing response to the media or the public, with wider spread systemic wrongdoing seemingly being uncovered and reported almost daily. This has led to something of a perceived (by police officers at least) media 'pile on', with policing as a profession being vilified, even further eroding public trust and confidence. Politicians of all stripes have jumped onboard these anti-police bandwagons, calling for reforms and inquiries into the fitness of the UK police service, and for officers to be dismissed easier by dispensing with existing due process. At an appearance before a house of commons select committee, Met Commissioner Sir Mark Rowley was subject to a personal attack on his character by Conservative party deputy chairman, Lee Anderson. This appalling spectacle was strong evidence of the contempt our politicians have for policing and its leaders and was a shameful display of behaviour by an elected politician. The impact of this relentless media reporting and political interventions has created a difficult culture for police officers, particularly those once again on its frontline. The policing profession has in effect been subject to repeat media and political vilification, often using unfounded rhetoric, which nevertheless in the current moral panic over police officers and their behaviour, results in mud generally sticking.

I have been outlining for some time the toxicity this environment has on the mental health and wellbeing of police officers and staff. Police officers are well used to being under the public and political spotlight, but this now feels much more like an interrogation lamp, as police behaviour and activity is relentlessly scrutinised, with armchair police commentators and 'talking heads' (most of whom are long retired police officers themselves) chucking in their tuppence worth with the very best hindsight analysis they are able to muster. Everyone it seems is now an expert in policing! There is a plausible risk that proactive policing itself will, in this seemingly never-ending environment of anti-police rhetoric, begin to experience a negative effect on what was once considered a highly effective approach to crime prevention, as officers increasingly feel that they no longer enjoy the level of political, public, and even internal support for proactively doing their jobs, terrified that they are one step away from appearing in a highly one-sided social media video potentially leading to misconduct or even criminal proceedings. The fear being that they would fall foul of the current negative sentiment being expressed both outside and, to some extent, even inside policing. I would in fact suggest that we have already begun to see the emergence of that trend in the UK, admittedly mainly due to the models of policing commonly invoked since the disastrous budget cuts by Cameron's government in 2010, whereby reactive response policing models now takes precedence in many forces over proactive anti-crime initiatives.

A similar situation became known in the United States as 'The Ferguson Effect', named after the town of Ferguson Missouri, where in 2014 an unarmed black male was shot and killed by a police officer who was defending himself against attack. The police officer was cleared of any wrongdoing. Nevertheless, the violence directed towards police officers and the large-scale civil unrest experienced in several urban areas across the United States that followed set in place a spiralling effect of repeated negative rhetoric, mainly expressed by politicians and 'social activists', directed towards the police. Policing as an institution was labelled as racist and discriminatory towards black communities, with officers experiencing increased hostility, violence, and even death. The resulting 'Ferguson Effect' saw law enforcement areas across the USA, significantly scale back on proactive policing activity such as stop and search (stop and frisk in the US), proactive traffic stops, and other anti-crime operations for fear they would be subject of unfounded complaints or even personally sued. Instead, it became safer to simply respond to calls for service (the reactive approach) as this presented far less risk as ultimately a report had been made by a member of the public triggering a reactive response and any follow up activity deemed appropriate. But no longer would police officers go out looking for suspicious persons, conduct stops, or do anything that may lead to complaints of civil rights violations.

Perhaps unsurprisingly, crime rates in many urban areas which had in fact been reducing over the previous years began to experience substantial increases including levels of homicide and serious violence. There can be little doubt that by stepping back from proactive policing tactics, criminals became all too aware and emboldened, and consequently crime levels increased, placing communities, particularly those in urban areas of high deprivation, at significantly greater risk of violent crime and victimisation. It was quickly established by US police chiefs at an emergency summit in Washington DC to address the rise in violent crime that, yes, proactive policing does have a role in reducing violent crime, and that the constant and unrelenting vilification of the police does indeed lead to such dysfunctional outcomes. Such a situation occurring in the UK would not, in the current climate, be all that surprising.

Policing is without a doubt a highly dangerous and unpredictable business. Perception of danger and our response to dangerous situations is a complex psychological phenomenon. It happens at both individual and collective level, and nowhere, perhaps other than the armed services during periods of active combat, is this more evident than in the context of police work. If our response to danger isn't properly understood and mitigated against whether that's through a sense of collective safety - or more commonly understood as 'safety in numbers' - or at an individual level in respect of personal fitness, training, and protective equipment then it can seriously inhibit the ability to properly do the job.

In addition to the physical dangers posed to police officers such as personal attacks, there are of course psychological dangers that have an impact. Exposure to traumatic incidents, of experiencing and witnessing unpleasant things can and will take its toll. Things that no 'ordinary' person will ever see or experience. This all adds to the emotional and psychological weight the officer carries on his or her shoulder each day. Policing is an unpredictable business, and you literally never know what you are going to experience from one day to the next. It is the only occupation on the planet where violence can, and will, be directed towards you solely on the basis of doing your job. Police officers step forward when others can step back. That's the deal, after all, it's the contract police officers sign with the public when they join. Policing remains as hazardous an occupation as it ever has been, that same sense of the unknown is ever present whenever a police officer steps outside the station or exits the patrol car.

Arguably, such dangers are easier to accept, or at the very least are acknowledged and understood as the principle occupational risk factors of frontline law enforcement professionals. More sophisticated equipment and training to mitigate against physical attacks along with the growing provision of wellbeing and trauma support are relatively straightforward to implement, and overall are considered to lead to a greater sense of occupational health, safety, and wellbeing. Other perceived dangers are however far harder to mitigate against, and a new far more pervasive risk, has over recent years begun to emerge.

The overt, and seemingly socially acceptable sentiment of public disdain, and at times expressions of sheer hatred directed towards policing in this country is at a level never experienced before. And this heightened level of distrust in and disdain for policing is, I suggest, steadily posing a new type of occupational danger to our frontline officers. It is being perpetrated principally by the media through their relentless, negative, and often sensationalist reporting and by political and other commentators who take any opportunity to criticise the police for any perceived wrongdoing. This new strain in the danger dynamic increases in police officers both the sense of physical danger to them at an individual level, not to mention the psychological effect on them in respect of their relationship with the profession itself. Although being warmly popular or well liked has never generally been part of the policing occupation, overt dislike and contempt for the police has now reached a worrying level. Public support for policing is now a rare expression, and this leads to additional risks faced by those working at the sharp end of policing. When discussing occupational stressors, officers cite much less often the operational risks and dangers such as personal violence or exposure to trauma. This might be surprising to some who might understandably assume that these matters would invoke the most personal stressors. Rather, poor, and inconsistent leadership, a sense of organisational injustice normally through negative experience of conduct or performance matters, and a general lack of wellbeing and leadership support are the big-ticket stressors that police officers will instead want to talk about.

Owing to many sections of the media as well as opportunist politicians of all stripes, police officers are more and more commonly portrayed as a convenient 'continuity oppressor' group, which, after all, in the current divisive era where the concept of identity politics reigns supreme is a useful label. In such a system, there must always be an oppressed victim group and a corresponding oppressor group. This can be dynamic in nature depending on the social issue of the day, for example transgender women as the oppressed and biological women as the oppressors, women as the oppressed and the patriarchy as the oppressors. The oppressed and oppressor groups are often interchangeable causing an ever-evolving shifting victim hierarchy, underpinned by the leftist concept of intersectionality. However, one amongst these various oppressor groups remains constant: the police service.

And this is not a new concept. When we look back to the introduction of Sir Robert Peel's 'New Police' in 1829, the orthodox historical view was that the Metropolitan Police were brought into being as previous policing structures were unfit for purpose, were unprofessional and prone to corruption, and did not provide anywhere near a proper service for the community. Revisionist historians would however disagree with this analysis, instead arguing that in the context of the industrial revolution, the ruling classes of the time, or as Marx describes them, the bourgeoisie, became worried and were so determined to maintain their own positions in contrast to the working class that Peel's new police were ushered in to protect such interests. In other words, the police were the oppressing agents of the state on behalf of the bourgeoisie with the working classes as the oppressed in this situation. It is clear to see how in the current social climate policing is again framed through this Marxist lens.

Attempts to challenge this image and shake off the oppressor label has seen the police service over recent years engage in a raft of misguided and wasteful activity, principally through asserting its stance on various social justice causes. This shift in police attitudes has been done to invite the public to witness the social conscience of the service when it comes to matters of injustice and discrimination.

The entire police organisation now seems to be in constant 'brace mode' having been labelled as racists, sexist, homophobic and misogynist so many times, always based on the actions of a relatively small minority of individuals. More worrying, the occupation now appears to have accepted its 'everything is bad' label and the impact this has on officers I suggest is significant and damaging.

No other occupation resulting from wrongdoing perpetrated by one of its members suffers such extreme and disproportionate treatment and public disdain. Have we demanded that all nurses are now re-vetted considering the horrific Lucy Letby case? Are the media and politicians stoking hatred and creating a climate of disdain and distrust for the entire nursing profession, vilifying its members based on the actions of one nurse however heinous her crimes? Of course not! And nor should they. Lucy Letby alone committed these crimes. Were her actions directly related to her occupation? Yes. And were they partly permitted by structural processes and a failure of systems and of individuals? Most probably. But thankfully we have not knee jerked in the way we did in cases involving the police. Nobody is being encouraged not to approach a nurse if they require medical assistance contrary to the advice given to women and girls not to approach lone male police officers following the horrific murder of Sarah Everard.

Sarah Everard's Murder

Whether a police officer or not, we were all shocked by the tragic murder of Sarah Everard. This sense of shock and disbelief at this young woman's abduction, rape, and murder was compounded by the fact that the killer was a serving Metropolitan police officer. It soon became evident that serious errors had been made in respect of the perpetrator, former PC Wayne Cousins, mainly relating to internal vetting failures and prior allegations against him not being properly investigated. The Metropolitan Police under its then Commissioner, Cressida Dick, acted swiftly, setting out an internal review and eventually an independent inquiry by Baroness Louise Casey was commissioned. But before pen could be put to paper, or any period of reflection undertaken, the self-flagellation and moral crusades within policing predictably began. One former Metropolitan Police officer and now convicted murderer had overnight apparently become representative of all male police officers. At best, male officers were now to be viewed with serious suspicion, as potential closet misogynists who urgently needed to 'check their thinking'. At worst they were also potential sexual predators. A campaign to help 'out' this horde of closet monsters began with posters and internal intranet communications encouraging staff to come forward and report male colleagues for displaying even the faintest whiff of misogynist or sexist behaviour, however dated these episodes may be. The message 'you will always be taken seriously' was the common strapline in such campaigns to encourage prospective reporters. I couldn't help but think that this contained an eerily similar tone to the non-crime hate incident reporting approach. It wasn't long before misconduct notices were flying around like confetti as male officers were accused of various transgressions, often allegations that had occurred years previously but had for some reason not been reported at the time. Nevertheless, these reports were pursued with gusto by professional standards departments, and some officers were rapidly suspended, disciplined, and even dismissed in many cases in respect of allegations that would previously have been assessed less severely.

The severity threshold for misconduct sanctions and dismissals had in effect been lowered owing to the prevailing fervent media and political rhetoric. Once again, the police service spectacularly knee jerked in their response to a perceived internal problem amidst a fever pitch climate. The usual anti-police lobby were demanding a parade of misogynist heads on spikes, and chief constables were more than happy to offer them up. And this was the moment many within the police service had been waiting for. Female leaders who had always considered men to be the natural enemy now had free reign to mete out justice, cynically using this young woman's murder to whip up anti-male rhetoric at any opportunity. The moral panic was well underway, with calls for male curfews to be established to protect lone females walking the streets at night. Feminist groups and many senior figures within policing had unbelievably conflated what had happened to Sarah with men wolf whistling or cat calling women on the street or on public transport and placed these innocuous behaviours on the same level as sexual assault. Posters were soon displayed on the London Underground encouraging the reporting of 'crimes' directed towards women and girls such as 'staring' and 'cat-calling'. Within the police service, and I'm sure in many other equally woke-fuelled organisations, men were to be recruited as female 'allies', an interesting term indeed, one normally associates with the context of war and conflict. The sub text of course being that if you're not with us you're against us. For some women, men were the enemy unless they could prove otherwise. The whole climate was designed to make 50% of the general population (and almost 80% of the police workforce) incredibly uncomfortable. 'You should feel uncomfortable' one senior female officer told me following a discussion on the topic. Say the wrong thing to the wrong person and it could easily be career over. Men did have to check their thinking after all, and with it their language. I will state very clearly that those subject of allegations of wrongdoing must be held to account. There is no question that those who have committed acts of gross misconduct, particularly as it relates to sexual harassment should be investigated, and if found guilty and where necessary dismissed. But the counterbalance to this is surely to ensure that due process is followed, that consistent and fair outcomes are made. Overtly soliciting complaints and lowering the severity bar due to a small handful of cases is simply disproportionate and does nothing for an already incredibly bashed and bruised workforce.

The current anti-police climate and damaging evidence-lacking rhetoric has astonishingly been fuelled just as much, if not more, by the bloated woke termites within policing as it has been by external anti-police commentators and opportunists. It has already started to cause a new psychological strain, an elevated risk of danger to our police officers both in a physical sense given the heightened level of anger and distrust directed towards them, and at a psychological level as they don their uniforms each day knowing that this is apparently the public sentiment. Being part of an occupation constantly under a barrage of negativity is not only unpleasant but is steadily eroding the sense of occupational pride in policing that so many once possessed. The cancellation of the British Bobby is near completion. The rate of attrition of new police entrants is at a worryingly high level. The blunt analysis by those wishing to deflect attention from themselves, including several PCC's and Chiefs, has been to lay the blame at the door of the relatively new PEQF process which some claim is directly responsible for this exodus. However, I've heard little discussion on the current climate that our new police recruits find themselves in. The job is surely hard enough to assimilate into without adding the relentless negative public discourse to the picture, not to mention the strain of poor leadership.

The Policing Minister, Chris Philp, recently announced that the Government will bring forward plans to ensure that Chief Constables will now be expected to dismiss officers found guilty of gross misconduct. In the most significant changes to the police misconduct processes in several years, Chief Constables or their Deputies will now chair gross misconduct hearings and if officers are found guilty will have the ability to automatically dismiss them. Until now, legally qualified chairs have presided over most misconduct panels and whilst they are able to invoke a dismissal sanction, are also able to dispose of cases by a number of other outcomes other than dismissal.

What the government plan to enact is not an entirely new process. Gross misconduct panels under previous misconduct regulations saw Chiefs as the sole decision maker in gross misconduct matters. Chiefs would sit akin to a judge, listening to both sides of the case before determining on guilt or innocence and then passing down the sentence. Among other reasons that this process was changed to a panel structure was that it presented a situation where misconduct process outcomes were inconsistent from force to force. For example, an officer convicted of drink driving in one force could face automatic dismissal, while an officer convicted of an identical offence in another force would face a lesser sanction such as a monetary fine or reduction in rank. This led to a high level of appeals being submitted by dismissed officers with a relatively high number later reinstated. Perhaps this new process will lead to more consistency, but its enactment is certainly something that should be closely monitored in the months to come. Indeed, the Independent Office for Police Conduct (IOPC) has expressed its concerns in respect of any change to the misconduct hearing process which places Chief Constables regularly in the position of 'judge and jury'. The Police Federation has expressed similar concerns.

And one of the main reasons for the government making such a significant change to the misconduct processes is the notion that making it easier to weed out the bad apples will lead to a restoration of public trust in policing. Many senior figures within policing will rub their hands at such a prospect. For me this is a questionable assumption, one that at best may only be partly correct. Yes, better systems to quickly dismiss those convicted of serious wrongdoing is critical (just look at the case of Metropolitan Police Commander Julian Bennet to see how ridiculously protracted these misconduct processes can be) but so many other root and branch reforms of the service need to be addressed, beginning I would suggest with re-establishing credible and capable police leadership, a quality the service is now seriously deficient in.

And whilst I reflect in this book mainly on the current UK context, it is evident that such negative rhetoric and disdain for policing is being experienced elsewhere in the world including the USA, Canada, and in some parts of Europe. This situation in fact appears to be part of a much wider western societal problem, one bound up in the general postmodernist repudiation of formal structures of power, authority, truth, and knowledge. A belief system in which the police, and authority in general, is considered functionally repressive.

In the meantime, the effect of the relentless negative climate of disdain and distrust here in the UK continues unabashed, and the job of our frontline police officers is made more dangerous and difficult as a direct consequence of such sustained negative rhetoric. Senior police leaders are rarely forthcoming in their support and defence of officers both at an internal and external level. Yes, this has been a challenging time for policing, but a basic message needs to be restated much more often by those at the top of the profession and delivered in a way that will overtly demonstrate support to their officers. That message being that most police officers – much like other public servants such as nurses, doctors, firefighters, and teachers – are decent hard-working human beings. And because human beings are sadly at times capable of doing very bad things, often without warning or the raising of red flags, it is regrettably impossible to completely mitigate against it.

Yes, systems can of course always be improved including enhancing recruitment and vetting processes as well as developing a swifter mechanism of addressing serious criminal allegations against officers. But essentially, most of our police officers, and this is certainly overwhelmingly my experience over 31 years, just want to do the best they can for their communities and go home safe and well at the end of every shift. Surely that is a basic human right and not much to expect from individuals who work hard each day to keep us safe. As the saying goes, society will invariably get the police service it deserves, and I fear that unless our society, particularly through those who purport to speak on its behalf, begin to show a better degree of respect and support for the police, then that is precisely what will happen.

CHAPTER 7

When it Hits the Fan, Experience Counts

As a senior police officer when the 'big one' happens it is invariably complete chaos to begin with. Information is coming at you thick and fast and from every angle, trying to get full and precise clarity and understanding of the situation is never easy, and knowing exactly what you have at your disposal in respect of available resources is rarely straightforward. In my experience, the difference between effective and ineffective command in leading major incidents is the ability to grab that chaos by the scruff of the neck and turn it into something that can be professionally and effectively responded to.

I undertook my College of Policing Public Order Gold (Strategic) Command course at Ryton near Coventry in 2018, and the next year attended the follow-up Multi Agency Gold Incident Command Course, colloquially known as the MAGIC course (sadly it did not entail learning how to pull rabbits out of hats or making people disappear, the latter would have been an especially nice skill to have mind you!). At that time, whilst I was keen to ensure I held the highest level of command accreditation in line with my rank, both courses were in fact a prerequisites for entry to the Strategic Command Course (this no longer being the case with the introduction of the new executive leadership program. In fact, no formal command accreditation is now required to become a chief police officer in the UK). But at that stage in my career, I had every intention of applying for the Strategic Command Course at some point in the future, and so needed to secure these professional qualifications. I was also always acutely aware that my own career path had no built-in shortcuts.

I found both courses to be appropriately challenging. The Gold public order course was tough, and not everyone passed, however I already had extensive experience of public order policing including as a trained public order Silver Commander and Silver Cadre for pan London (Operation Benbow) public order deployments. I was therefore quietly confident I'd be fine and passed the course on first sitting. The MAGIC course however was a completely different experience as it comprised of police learning alongside partner agencies. This included other 'blue light' services alongside local authority partners which made for a diverse mix of experience, knowledge, and perspectives. All participants were at least in theory qualified to act in a gold capacity in respect of their own agency, and the purpose of this course was to ensure that at a strategic level a joint understanding and common approach amongst partners to civil emergency response was achieved.

The course itself lasted a week, was generally enjoyable, and at the very least provided collective awareness of the roles and responsibilities of the different agencies in the context of a civil emergency. At the end of the week, I was left thinking that it had been helpful in developing my knowledge and understanding of civil emergency management, and that ultimately it was a good one to have on my CV. Little did I know that in just over a year from then I would be put to the test as a multi-agency gold commander for a significant major incident.

On 12th August 2020 I was working at home at the height of the COVID pandemic when my mobile rang. It was one of my Chief Inspectors telling me that there had been a major passenger train derailment in Aberdeenshire, north-east Scotland, and several fatalities were predicted. I immediately made my way to my office, at that point not realising that I wouldn't be back home for several days.

To be clear, I have no intention of describing the intricate details of the train derailment itself. I am acutely aware of the sensitivities that exist. More I want to take you through the first few hours of 'chaos', the days that followed, and how I tried to put in effect solutions to deal with the various challenges that faced me as the gold commander. Essentially, experience was everything.

The first thing I did on arriving at work was to take 15 minutes alone in my office. I needed to make sense of what we were dealing with. I was the only available MAGIC accredited Gold and so knew I would be leading the strategic response to this one. I also knew that this was quickly developing into a significant major incident and so I needed to get my thinking and composure straight in preparation for such a substantial command role. I also knew that once I opened that office door I would be pulled in every direction until I had set the necessary structures in place.

I'll readily acknowledge that whilst some of these initial steps I will outline might seem obvious when read in the cold light of day, when you are in the midst of chaos it's really easy to forget the most basic principles and your training, including my recently completed MAGIC course. Taking that 15 minutes allowed me to reflect on these necessary critical first steps and set out a plan in my own mind about what I needed to do, what my priorities were, and critically, who I needed alongside me to make it all work.

Setting out some basic strategic intentions was my first task. I was conscious that the police incident officer - a thankfully experienced inspector – was at the scene and that I had a chief inspector en route who would assume the tactical command role. Therefore, I considered it crucial that those leaders at the sharp end of our response were aware of my initial strategy to help shape and support their own priorities and decision-making. Having briefed the on-call ACC, I then devised a command structure. This is where really knowing who your people are, their strengths and abilities, comes into play, the term square pegs and square holes is certainly relevant here, and thankfully at that time I had an excellent team of Chief Inspectors and Inspectors as well as police staff colleagues around me who made the task a reasonably straightforward one.

Having set the command responsibilities and communicated my strategy, it was important to consider the communications process. Control of information and intelligence is a critical step (appearing first on the joint emergency services interoperability principles joint decision model) and gaining that single version of the truth in respect of the situation is critical. I was fortunate that I had invested the time over the years to build my networks in local forces and had also developed positive working relationships with several non-policing partners. At times like these, knowing some of these key players in other agencies is a massive benefit, and saves a lot of time. Fortunately, I personally knew my local Police Scotland counterpart, the divisional commander in the north-east division, and we quickly arranged a call to set out command protocols and establish at strategic level a joint understanding of the situation. Formal communication and briefing arrangements including setting up the strategic coordinating group processes with partners was established, and media and other strategies were put in place.

Around two hours in, it was clear that the incident was indeed significant in nature with several deceased persons confirmed, a remote and challenging incident scene to manage, with the need to consider resources and command resilience for days and perhaps even weeks to come. Political and press interest was beginning to mount, and as the Gold commander, this was now coming at me thick and fast. My dilemma at that point was whether to personally attend the scene or not. This is the difficult balance that strategic commanders need to strike. To be accessible, visible (paying due regard to whom you need to be accessible and visible to) but simultaneously to not intrude on or interfere with the decision making of commanders at tactical and operational level. This isn't easy for most of us who have been in policing for a long time, who, like me, are hardwired with the instinct to get there and get stuck in. This is difficult to resist. My decision was to make for the scene (over two hours away by road) but that my key objectives in doing so were to i) personally touch base with the tactical commander and his team to ensure they had everything they needed, ii) gain an appreciation of the scale of the incident as, whilst I had viewed ariel images, I felt there was no substitute for seeing this for myself. After all, in the days to come I'd be expecting my people to work long and difficult hours there, so I felt it was important to see it for myself. And iii) it also gave me an opportunity to meet some of the key partners on site and check the welfare provisions being put in place. I have learned from previously major incidents I've been involved in that welfare, feeding, and generally ensuring that your people are looked after from the start is a key element to how people will perform, and in turn how professionally the whole situation will be dealt with.

So, I went and saw it for myself. In that lovely summer evening in 2020, I witnessed the full devastation of a passenger train derailment in person for the first time, the tragic loss of life it had claimed, and this all having occurred in an otherwise breathtakingly beautiful part of the Scottish countryside. For me this made it surreal and horrifying in equal measures. The scene was as busy as I had expected it to be, there was a lot of emergency service personnel present, each getting on with their respective priorities. Other partners including the local authority, Rail Accident Investigation Branch, and representatives from the rail industry were all present and they too were getting on with the task at hand. Yes, the mood was sombre, the scene was challenging, people were busy, but there was no sense of chaos. That much was clear. Everyone was getting on with their work, it looked and felt controlled and orderly, and everyone I spoke to was clear about the emergency services priorities and their respective organisational responsibilities. And this was only a few hours into the incident response, not a long time considering the remoteness and inaccessibility of the location, and seriousness and complexity of the incident itself. So, I did what I had set out to do, spoke to who I needed to speak to, and then made for the nearby police station which would serve as my command base for the next week.

One of the many questions I pondered in the hours to come during what transpired to be a mostly sleepless night in my Aberdeen hotel room, was what precisely had managed to tame the chaos?

Had I just been lucky? Had everyone simply been ready to spring into gear and respond so professionally to such a significant and challenging major incident? I wasn't entirely sure, but those thoughts were soon overtaken with other priorities, including how to achieve separate meetings the following day with two Transport secretary's from different governments (which trust me, wasn't easy and which was actually in hindsight something of a distraction). So, I put the chaos question to the back of my mind for the time being.

The days ahead were long, the job of coordinating activity at the scene, ensuring I had the resources required (and the budget!), dealing with lots of media enquiries, and ensuring I was available for the battle rhythm of meetings and briefings that would take place throughout the day were all crucial activities. I also made time to visit the incident scene once a day for the next week and had taken the decision to appoint on scene trauma support, chaplaincy, and a dedicated police federation representative to deal with any pressing personnel or welfare issues. Aside from the distressing nature of the incident, most of my officers were staying away from home for days on end, and so welfare and on-site support provision was a key measure I put in place. This daily visit, only for an hour or so, allowed me to check in with the key individuals, to show visible leadership to my team, and to sense check that my understanding through briefings was indeed accurate. Again, always careful not to intrude on the decision making of the other commanders present.

One of the things I had learned from previous large-scale incidents I've led was that ensuring you have the right level of personal support is critical. As such, I had appointed a gold support role who was a temporary chief inspector and himself a highly experienced officer to that position. This individual knew me very well, understood how I worked, what my thinking was likely to be on any given issue, and was usually a step ahead of me. I also had excellent dedicated media support provided to me and this took a significant amount of pressure away from me given how understandably intrusive the media had become. Train crashes are not thankfully common occurrences, and the media and political interest and associated community tensions were significant.

I was also fortunate that I had a very supported chief officer team. The ACC visited the scene, again not to become involved in any decision making, but to support me and to check that I had everything I needed. The deputy chief constable kept in touch via phone and was also incredibly supportive. Neither got involved in decision-making at any level, and this trust and confidence was something I really appreciated. Frankly, not all chief officers would have been able to keep their hands off!

We also received a visit to the scene by His Majesty King Charles (at that time Prince Charles) who was in residence at nearby Balmoral Castle. Whilst we did have to consider the usual security provisions, the visit itself was low key, with His Majesty simply wanting to view the scene for himself and visit members of the local community and emergency service personnel working at the site. I thought this was an especially nice touch and demonstrated the often-unseen compassionate nature of our Royal Family in such times of crisis.

At the appropriate point, I was able to stand the formal command structure down. The scene was still 'live', but the job had moved to one of scene preservation pending uplift of the derailed locomotives, in itself a highly complex technical task. At that point, along with my command team, I was able to properly reflect on how it had all gone as we prepared for a structured debrief and the lessons learned process. By sheer fluke, someone asked if I wanted to view a video of the first multi-agency meeting that had taken place at the scene which had been led by my inspector, the initial police incident officer. He had impressively had the foresight to record this meeting on his body worn video camera. I watched as he diligently and calmly followed to the letter the joint emergency services interoperability principles (JESIP) in the format of his briefing, ensuring a joint understanding of the incident was present whilst relaying my initial gold strategy to his emergency service counterparts as they set about the rescue and recovery phase of the incident.

And that's when it struck me! It was this calm and professional approach that had helped set the tone of the entire emergency service response. It had ensured a truly collaborative first responder operating climate, applying the key elements of interoperability in a real time operational major incident scenario. Experience is what had tamed the chaos and was in fact an excellent demonstration of sound operational leadership in an otherwise high-pressure, confused, and chaotic environment. To say I was truly impressed at something which, until that point had been acknowledged but which otherwise had not been given the credit it deserved towards the overall success of the operation, would be an understatement. Simple? Yes. Effective? Highly!

So, what did I learn in my first (and what turned out to be my last) outing as a multi-agency gold commander for a major civil emergency, and what advice could I offer to those who might find themselves in a similar position? There are probably three key things I'd recommend to those within policing reading this and who may find themselves in this position. Firstly, do take that initial time out to take some breaths, gather as much of your initial briefing together in your own mind and begin to map out your working strategy. Do not underestimate the importance of getting that strategy circulated as soon as you are able, even if it's not a work of art, it can always be developed and updated later. It really does add value and assist colleagues who are at the front end of the response. This was confirmed during the structured debrief, that receiving the gold strategy early in the process made the role of the police incident officer and tactical commander a much more straightforward one, especially in the initial hours of the incident.

Second, get a command structure underway as soon as you can. As with the initial strategy, you can always amend it as you go, but assigning key roles and responsibilities to commanders takes the pressure off and allows people to get on with the many tasks that need completed. Aligned to this is knowing your people well. This might not always be possible, especially if it's not your own command area, or if you've only just arrived. But it does help, so if this is something you are struggling with, don't be afraid to ask a trusted colleague to help you out in this regard.

Thirdly, make sure you have a proportionate level of support around you. This effectively becomes your inner circle and will comprise of those individuals who you will spend a great deal of time with over the days to come. Having a staff officer or gold support function, tactical advisor if required, a loggist to help record and track your decisions, and any other support you feel necessary will make you a much more effective multi-agency gold commander. Some commanders are reluctant to appoint to these roles, thinking that it ultimately means less boots on the ground in the operational response if abstracting to such support functions. This in my view is narrow thinking, as failing to do so will ultimately make you much busier than you need to be and invariably you will be less effective in your own role. Part of these support roles is being able to gatekeep access to you as the gold commander. In the first couple of days particularly, everyone will want a piece of you, and it is not always possible or appropriate to speak to or meet with everyone. Good personal support, and a well set out command structure in general, will greatly assist with this aspect, ensuring that you don't become completely swamped and overwhelmed with distracting issues.

Each major incident and civil emergency will of course be different, and so agility is always required. The police will not always be the primary agency depending on the scenario itself, albeit policing always invariably has a crucial role to play. However, regular attendance at local resilience forums, participating in testing and exercising events, investing time to get to know your partners (and your own people), and undertaking appropriate command accreditation will collectively make the command role a far less stressful one when that 'big one' finally does arrive. Overall, sound operational leadership experience is of critical importance in respect of those involved in key command positions. In this instance, I was incredibly fortunate that I had an exceptional team around me. They were *my* team, many of them I had even personally promoted and so knew their competence and suitability. For that, I will always be grateful.

CHAPTER 8

The College of Policing: A Unique Experience

Having served as an operational superintendent for six years, in 2022 I began to seek out new challenges. I applied for and was successful in gaining a promoted post to the College of Policing in the newly created role of National Performance Improvement Lead. Despite all the challenges and dysfunctional culture within policing I have described, I always have, and in whatever role, tried my best to drive forward and achieve the best possible service and standards for the public. This has meant keeping a close watch on performance, how many crimes we were solving, what our response times looked like, especially for emergency calls, and what our victims feedback told us. I'm the first to admit that I was passionate about this area, and often found myself slipping into overbearing mode at times, especially when junior colleagues were not completely on their game or didn't know their business. I always however took some pride in striking the correct balance between leading people effectively and being able to hold their feet to the fire when required for failing performance. That is what the public expect, and as a superintendent, I was being paid well to ensure it was being done. So, when the job at the College of Policing came up, I thought it would be right up my street.

My first impressions of the College were reasonably positive. This was the first role I'd had in my career which was designated as home working. My boss was based in London while I was in Glasgow, but the wonder of Microsoft Teams made all things possible in the post COVID world. The box of I.T. goodies arrived on time, and the first couple of meetings with my new boss and small College team were generally positive encounters. The problem however was that nobody really seemed to have a clue what we should be doing. This was a new role and entirely new offering by the College of Policing to forces who were underperforming, either as assessed by the policing inspectorate (HMIC) or the Home Office performance scorecard which assessed individual forces against crime performance outcomes. So, in strategic terms at least, the remit seemed clear. What did not exist however was any real sense of direction by either the College themselves, or indeed by the Home Office who were directly funding the endeavour by way of a specific grant arrangement. After the short honeymoon period had ended, I became rather impatient, and ready to get out there and assist forces in any way I could. After all, in many respects, policing was then, and still is, in a bad way, and I was keen to get out there and do my bit in trying to reverse some of the decline in performance and standards. But, getting this done, particularly at any speed, was simply not the College way of doing business. In policing, you generally must respond quickly to get things done, whether that is to address matters internally or externally. The hierarchy works well in this regard, allowing tasks to be assigned and delegated and for hard deadlines to be set. No such culture exists at the College of Policing. The organisation itself is a sort of quango I suppose, a company limited by guarantee and financially propped up by the Home Office. A Chief Executive Officer leads the circa 700 strong organisation, with the appointee generally being a retired chief constable, (the present incumbent previously led the Avon and Somerset force at a time when his officers were seen to stand idly by whilst Black Lives Matter protestors ran amok in Bristol, ripping down statues before depositing one of them into a nearby river). Now, you would be forgiven for thinking that the College of Policing comprises mostly of police professionals as its title might suggest. It doesn't. Most of the workforce are in fact civil servants, with a much smaller compliment of police officers like me who go there on secondment for anything up to three years. The first thing that unsettled me was just how disjointed the organisation is. It is a relatively small outfit, but it is vastly complex in its structures, with a tremendous amount of duplication going on. Often, the left hand seldom knows what the right hand is up to. It is also spectacularly bloated in respect of leadership structure, especially considering its modest size. It has a CEO, Deputy CEO, a multitude of Directors and their deputies, heads of functions and a plethora of managers. But despite this inflated leadership structure, there is little evidence of a functioning hierarchy. Everyone just seems to do their own thing with apparently very little direction. And police rank means absolutely nothing. As a chief superintendent, I had no staff responsibility, nobody I could assign tasks to, no personal support for administration or to help with travel and accommodation bookings. Nothing. Being in such a senior police rank meant very little at the College. In fact, I discovered early on that the post I occupied was originally designed for a civil servant, but owing to the fact that a chief super would have more professional credibility when engaging with forces it was progressed in that direction instead.

But my main observation of the College of Policing was how little those I engaged with there understood anything about the realities of policing. As I said, most were career civil servants of varying grades, some had been at the College for substantial periods, while others were regularly recycled in from other government departments such as the Home Office or Ministry of Justice. Regardless, except for a small handful I encountered, it was evident that very few really understood policing. Some had backgrounds in social science, law, or policy, but none really understood the day to day functions of policing, its structures, challenges, or culture. This really surprised me, and it was the first red flag that the College of Policing may well not be the organisation I had hoped to work for. Direction and tasking were poor, and I tried to put structures in place to address this. After all, there was no shortage of forces needing or indeed asking for our support. But we were never quick to respond to anything, and whenever I tried to move things on, I was told 'remember, you're working to College time now'. I heard that phrase often over the next nearly 12 months. So, I was in the position as a chief superintendent, where I had no staff, was provided next to no direction, and was working in a general culture of humdrum and 'slow as we go'. I simply had not been used to that. There was no proper strategic feel about the place, everyone just seemed to amble from one pointless meeting to another without achieving much of anything.

I tried to devise structures and processes to ensure we had some sense of order and measurable outputs (not that the Home Office seemed overly concerned about their investment), and I was marginally successful. After some months, I eventually managed to visit my first force to provide an element of support in crime investigation. Every time I needed something from within the College however to support me whether it was analytical support or administrative assistance, I had to put my case forward and often join the back of a queue. It will be of no surprise then to know that the College of Policing has found itself in the government's crosshairs more than once, recently during Suella Braverman's tenure as Home Secretary. She had identified them as being a largely inefficient and expensive outfit, and of being at the centre of the police woke agenda. At one time there were apparently serious discussions among Home Office officials about closing the College of Policing down. I have to say that if the organisation closed tomorrow, UK policing would barely register it, such is the lack of contribution and relevance it has in a wider context. The College is in my experience an echo-chamber, and very little of what it says, does, or produces significantly resonates with day to day policing structures. It is largely irrelevant, and the handful of key functions it does possess such as public order, firearms, and search training, delivered by police officer secondees in any case, could be undertaken just as effectively, if not better, elsewhere. I had heard many dissenting voices about the College in the years leading up to me joining it. The organisation was often referred to tongue in cheek by some as 'The Collapse of Policing', a label, that having spent almost a year with the organisation, I do not now consider an unkind or inaccurate description in the least.

During my time at the College of Policing I had discovered through first hand experience, and to my personal disappointment, that the organisation, rather than provide any direction and focus for positive policing reform, and with it an opportunity to help deliver change myself in the final years of my own police career, had turned out not in any way to be the solution to the problems that pervade British policing, but rather seemed to me to be a fundamental part of the problem. Politically left-leaning civil servants run the College of Policing, the College provide guidance and, in some instances, mandated codes of practice that influence how forces deliver policing across the country. It is the nucleus of the woke agenda that has infected policing so badly, in some ways we could describe it as patient zero. The amount of resource and effort that go into the DEI agenda at the College is substantial. And very little of this makes policing any more effective at catching criminals or keeping people safe. It is a racket that has gotten well out of hand. Indeed, careers in policing have been made on the back of the DEI agenda. Not only have those considered to be underrepresented been elevated to positions many were simply incapable of performing, but the DEI enterprise has seen a lot of investment by way of new roles and departments being established in forces to drive the message forward. Senior leaders are having their feet held to the fire much more for delivering DEI action plans than they are for improving their operational crime performance.

For many of us within policing, in my case recently retired, it is so evident what needs to be done to reform the profession and what changes would resonate most with the public. We need a hard factory reset and a return first and foremost to our conventional crime prevention and detection functions. My fear is that the woke madness is now far too widespread, and to paraphrase Christopher Hitchens once more, the termites have now burrowed in so deeply that it may be impossible to eradicate them. You see, the reforms needed would require those at the top of policing, including those at the College of Policing and National Police Chiefs Council, to admit that the emperor is indeed naked and has been so for a considerable time. That the harmful DEI ideologies that have occupied so much of their time and energy were in fact at best just wasteful endeavours, and that those who truly believe in these DEI orthodoxies, akin to a religious experience for some, need to give them up. Those who never really believed, but who embraced them anyway for fear of cancellation would similarly need to admit that they had been wrong as the reset button was hit. This group are in many ways worse than the true believers, as they cynically embrace the concepts so as not to rock the boat or interrupt their own career progression. I have known many.

Not everything about policing is bad. There remain some excellent, passionate, and dedicated people there. Many understand full well that the current climate of woke, mediocracy, and poor public service run rife, but they turn up anyway and strive to do their best regardless. I have been critical here on many occasions of police leadership, and rightly so. These are after all those privileged, well remunerated, group of people running police forces up and down the country. And for the most part, they are doing a dreadful job of it. And it isn't only me making this claim, just take a look at some of the HMIC PEEL inspection reports - the acronym PEEL standing for police efficiency, effectiveness, and legitimacy, a methodology used to inspect forces annually across a raft of distinct areas such as investigating crime, responding to the public, and, managing offenders - which are available online. You will see that the policing inspectorate are just as critical in their assessment in respect of many issues including a lack of effective leadership. I won't rehearse the reasons why I consider the state of leadership to be so spectacularly poor, hopefully I've made this point clear enough. There are some very good and decent chief officers out there who occasionally do speak up and go against the grain and who are at least trying to achieve the mission reset that policing in the UK so desperately requires, Steve Watson Chief Constable of Greater Manchester Police being one such figure. But they are regrettably in a serious minority, and for many their further career progression depends entirely on them obediently towing the party line in respect of the DEI mantra.

Technical ability, strategic perspective and possessing a rounded policing and leadership pedigree have become for many chief constables less desired qualities than blind and absolute adherence to the DEI ideology. And the reason I focus on leadership so much is that the woke chiefs and their entourage are promoting and advancing those in their own 'progressive' image, those who either genuinely believe in the DEI liberal left ideologies, or who do a good job at convincing those around them that they really do. Liberal left woke ideologies are now more often put forward in a highly intolerant way. As comedian Rob Schneider puts it, it is intolerance dressed up as good manners. It is a fundamentalist ideology that does not respond well to challenge, the expression of opposing orthodoxies, or anything else that threatens its narrative and undermines the racket that DEI has become. More worrying, we now see both within and outside of policing, those brave souls who dare speak up and do so contrary to the prevailing identity politics narrative of the day, are effectively vilified and eventually cancelled. No discussion or debate is permitted, they are simply shut down. Cancellation is the term we hear more often used in this regard, normally referring to those in high profile positions such as celebrities or politicians. These are the people who dare speak up and go against the grain of what is considered the prevailing group-think opinion. One such person cancelled with devastating consequences to his life and professional career is Graham Linehan.

Graham Linehan

For those who don't know, Graham Linehan, is the Irish comedy writer responsible for television programmes such as Father Ted and the IT Crowd. Linehan became involved in the thorny issue of transgender rights and spoke out against trans women (biological men) being immediately provided access to conventional safe spaces for women and girls, a debate topic frequently played out in the world of politics, broadcasting and elsewhere. He took the position that he strongly opposed access by trans men to women's spaces such as changing rooms and toilets, and also spoke up against children being permitted at a young age to not only identify themselves as another sex, but to undergo treatment regimes in response such as puberty blocking medication and in some cases irreversible surgery.

For his trouble, the notoriously offence-taking and militant woke rent-a-mob soon kicked into cancellation mode, attacking Linehan on social media platforms and labelling him as 'transphobic'. The onslaught was relentless. In a brave attempt to provide some context, and to express more fully his concerns and opinions, Linehan engaged conventional media platforms and provided a number of interviews where he candidly and eloquently discussed his concerns about the current trans ideology and how this was beginning to affect children in particular . Sadly, this did not help, and in some ways accelerated the cancellation agenda against him. No matter what he said, Linehan was now labelled an intolerant right-wing bigot, someone who risked his career and livelihood by speaking out on issues that if we are honest, the silent majority only dared think about. In doing so his upcoming Father Ted, the Musical, due to debut in London's west end was cancelled, along with several other planned appearances and engagements. Some of Linehan's long standing friends, particularly those in the entertainment industry, failed to support him publicly, leaving the writer completely isolated. And his heinous crime? Voicing his opinion, an opinion shared by many others including medical doctors, scientists, and politicians. Whether you agree with Linehan's views or not is irrelevant. What is of deep concern is the systematic way his career was dismantled by those who failed to support or defend his right to free speech. That is in so many ways worse than the twitter pitchfork brigade who came calling for his head.

Linehan's experience although high profile given his status, is sadly now not an uncommon one. Many others who have dared to express an opinion that is considered even mildly controversial risk the same pile-on by the ever ready and watchful baying woke rent-a-mob. Debate and discussion are no longer permitted in respect of certain topics, particularly if you are planning to disagree or provide an alternative perspective to the espoused narrative. This is the end of free speech, and aside from the devastating effects and heartache suffered by people like Graham Linehan (and I hope I have done his story justice here) many more are likewise suffering with some even being criminalised for expressing similar sentiments, or at the least having their details held in police data files as the perpetrator of a non-crime hate incident. It is the very hallmark of a totalitarian society, one which seeks to control, and moderate speech based on a perceived injury to feelings. The simple fact being that you cannot engage in debate in respect of controversial topics without the risk of causing someone somewhere an element of offence. It is impossible. I am not for one minute suggesting that there should be no consequences whenever someone deliberately goes out of his or her way to cause serious offence, and the motivator for that behaviour is based on an individual's protected characteristics. In many cases this may even constitute a criminal act depending on the circumstances. But these situations are almost always obvious to most people, and amount to significantly more than mild offence-causing remarks or indeed transgressing from the common narrative be that trans rights or any other social cause. Overt racist or homophobic remarks directed at an individual, especially when accompanying other criminal behaviour are examples of where one can often establish hate as a motivating factor for example. The police have been prosecuting these type of offences for decades. But the threshold has seemingly plummeted drastically, where the mere suggestion of offence being caused to anyone, whether the intended target or not, will often trigger a formal police investigation. I mention Linehan's case for two reasons: firstly, it is a good example of how intolerant the woke warriors have now become to any challenge and to show the lengths they are prepared to go to in order to cancel critics of their ideology. Secondly, to point out that this tactic is no longer simply applicable to high profile celebrities. Many others, including those in policing, now find themselves suffering a similar fate for speaking out against the DEI orthodoxy. Even the mildest critique is often treated akin to an act of blasphemy. Careers have been prematurely halted, dissenters of DEI soon find that they are labelled as 'phobes' or 'ists' of one type or another, and those around them, even although they may quietly think the same, will readily turn their backs for fear of being tarnished. The cancel culture is very real and is becoming more sinister by the day.

CHAPTER 9

What about the Public?

By far the worst thing about the spectacular decline of our police force is the impact it has had on the public. After all, the average member of the public may not fully appreciate to what extent the police have imploded, and, for the most part, this book is written for them. Those within policing will hopefully appreciate it too, and most will be fully aware of the woes facing policing and may nod their heads accordingly. Others, fewer in number I suspect, within the service will be utterly enraged that I have pulled the curtain back on a dysfunctional regime, on doing so revealing many of them relentlessly polishing their virtue signalling halos. To those people I say, take a good look in the mirror I've held up to you and decide whether its worth continuing along the dangerous and damaging path you tread.

I'm sure it will astonish many to learn that the public are more often very much secondary in strategic police decision making in the current era. Whether it's the continuous obsession with DEI, securing better levels of 'representation', or deciding which protected group deserves more attention against hurt feelings or offensive tweets this week, most of the law-abiding public simply do not feature. Instead, the public have become acceptable pawns in the diversity agenda, one which accepts a lowering in standards and the promotion of the mediocre for the 'greater good'. Policing is less about high standards and public service now and substantially more about its DEI and social conscience optics. The service has found itself locked in a vicious cycle whereby the more negative publicity it gets (some it deserves and some it does not), the more it focusses on reputational protection through ill-considered short-term strategies. And those strategies rarely talk to the need to restore the mission of crime fighting or protecting the public. And a significant element of such a self-perpetuating cycle are of course the police decision makers, themselves largely ill-equipped to solve these problems. You only have to look at those senior officers regularly paraded in front of the iconic Scotland Yard signage when things go wrong, and like me, I'm sure you will agree that these individuals generally inspire little confidence among the public let alone command respect and credibility within their own ranks. The term lions led by lambs always springs to mind.

You Reap What You Sow: A Case in Point

My last operational role prior to joining the College of Policing was as a divisional Superintendent in British Transport Police. I transferred to BTP several years ago and proudly served the once highly effective specialist police force in a number of roles and locations across the country. Crime performance in BTP was always a key priority, and its senior leaders were personally held to account for crime levels and detection rates. BTP's chief officers were laser focussed on the service provided by the force to the travelling public and those working on the railways and relentlessly drove performance and standards to ensure those at the top of the organisation in senior positions fully understood and delivered this objective. If your crime performance as a senior leader responsible for a geographic area was not acceptable, you were out of that role and someone else was swiftly appointed to do a better job. It was ruthless, the culture applied a lot of pressure to deliver results, and rightly so. Chief Superintendents and Superintendents are paid a lot of money to deliver the best possible policing outcomes for the public, and for ensuring that those they lead perform to the highest possible standards. Former BTP Chiefs like Andy Trotter demanded that his senior leaders, those of superintendent and above rank, possessed a credible operational pedigree. If you couldn't provide evidence of a positive track record of delivering results, then you need not apply. BTP's operational crime performance was consistently amongst the best in the country, and this did not happen by accident. The force made the determination that ensuring high levels of operational policing standards was its number one priority. Senior officers were directly held to account for this through rigorous performance meetings and those wearing superintendents' crowns were expected to know their business, and that was right and proper. The square pegs for square holes ideology was, at that point in time at least the prevailing system of merit. And it worked, the crime statistics proved it. Leaders were appropriately selected and posted purely on their suitability and experience to undertake the roles. It was that simple. Meritocracy not mediocrity.

In 2021, a new chief constable took the helm at BTP, this time an individual much more focused on DEI issues than any of her predecessors, particularly the progression and promotion of female officers in the service. Indeed, she proclaimed her vision to enhance the proportion of female senior leaders in one of her first internal communication messages on becoming the BTP Chief. Not long into her appointment, the new chief began to openly conclude, a little prematurely in my judgement, that parts of the organisation resembled an 'old boys club', that promotion systems were unfair and lacked transparency, and that there were simply too few women in the top BTP jobs. And so, the new chief constable set about reforming this old boys club she had inherited. One of her principal objectives towards creating the necessary changes was to oversee the promotion of more women to leadership positions and to increase their representation within specialist departments such as public order and firearms throughout the organisation. In doing so, there would inevitably be some capable and experienced male candidates passed over, many of whom I knew had been undertaking lengthy periods of temporary promotion beforehand and who, in my eyes at least, had proven their capability and suitability for permanent promotion. And so, these people became necessary casualties of the DEI agenda, in some instances leapfrogged by female officers some of whom were purported to be less qualified for positions.

Nevertheless, the chief constable had begun to achieve her ambition of greater representation of women in the senior ranks of BTP, and doing so was most certainly her prerogative as the newly installed leader of the organisation. Yes, there would of course be some internal casualties, but the chief had clearly made an assessement that organisational change was needed, and like any change of this nature there would be winners and losers. After all, you can't make a DEI omelette without breaking some male eggs. Well, in many ways it really did matter. Not only did it cause a predictable degree of ill feeling and resentment on the part of those who felt a sense of injustice at being passed over for positions, but around the same time BTP's crime performance began to trend in the wrong direction. Crime, particularly violent, sexual crime, and robbery started to increase in many parts of the country, and correspondingly arrest and detection rates began to slump. In all fairness, I do not lay the blame for the decline in BTP's crime performance entirely at the door of the chief's decision to promote more women (albeit in doing so overlooking many capable men in my view) or for her focus on DEI. There were other factors at play including a lack of organisational focus and grip on operational performance monitoring more generally. However, in my assessment, the appointment of inexperienced leaders along with a near singular focus (obsession) with DEI issues contributed at least in part to the force failing to get an early grip of its declining operational performance and standards. I witnessed first-hand how at force performance boards some of those who had been catapulted into key positions simply did not possess the experience or background to address these challenges we faced to improve our crime performance. As I've said previously, when the chips are down and decisive operational decision-making is required, those who are not experienced enough and do not have enough to draw on through their own previous policing and operational leadership exposure will seriously struggle to turn things around quickly enough to make a difference. And this is precisely in my assessment what happened in BTP. Many of the newly installed leaders, whilst perhaps ticking some diversity boxes, did not possess the experience or track record to address these emerging crime performance problems. Crimes of robbery, sexual offences, and disorderly behaviour particularly in BTP's London jurisdiction have spiralled to worrying levels. The relentless focus on non-policing matters such as internal DEI campaigning has caused the force to take its eye off the ball. This may suit the wider agenda of enhancing female representation, but it has apparently done noting to enhance BTP's operational performance or for its service to the travelling public. Until the BTP hierarchy, many of whom are in fact themselves retired senior officers from the Metropolitan Police Service (make of that what you will), shift its focus onto the things that really matter and begin to appoint the right people to the right roles, things are sadly unlikely to change.

The BTP scenario, and it is a situation surely reflected in forces across the country, demonstrates how the obsession with DEI box ticking can often come at a cost, that of providing the best police service for the public. This is worrying and goes to the heart of what is wrong with British policing; its focus and priorities are outright wrong. The public are getting a massively raw deal, as collective self-indulgence within police leadership runs wild. If a force or chief constable determines that for example there is a lack of female officers in senior positions (providing that is a correctly stated fact, and I'm not always sure it is) then that is fine. Look to address this by putting systems in place which better exposes and prepares up and coming female officers for the skills they will need in the future to undertake senior policing roles. But what you cannot and should not do is to discriminate against competent and capable men in the process. That is not acceptable, neither for the individuals concerned, nor for the public whom policing is meant to serve. Whilst the prevailing mantra as it relates to white middle-aged men in policing may well be 'male, pale, and stale', to dismiss an entire group in favour of those possessing different genitalia is surely the ultimate form of discrimination. It is in fact a highly overt process of achieving equity, or equality of outcome, that most pernicious element of the DEI triangle. It is done in plain sight by those who firmly believe the argument to be on their side, who flash the badge of oppression in the face of anyone who dares to speak up. It is hugely destructive and does nothing to provide a professional and effective police service.

British Bobby, Where Art Thou?

No one is suggesting that the cures for the various ills of British policing rest with a return to the Dixon of Dock Green era of policing. The days of clipping miscreants around the ears and of officers patrolling largely on foot are over. However, it remains evident that many people no longer recognise the British Police service from even twenty or thirty years ago, and they are correct in this observation. Policing has changed, and in many ways not for the better. While advances in science and technology, investigative practices such as DNA and the widespread deployment of CCTV have, at least in theory, made policing and investigating crime more effective, many more aspects of British policing have gone badly wrong. The previously hardwired concept of the crime-fighting mission has all but evaporated, as police officers spend so much of their time dealing with the demand heaped on them by other public services, their numbers have been vastly cut thanks to the Cameron and May administration in 2010, and the police leadership is far too timid and inexperienced to stand up to political interference or to stop the infestation of identity politics which has so badly dented the impeccable reputation for neutrality and impartiality that British Policing once possessed. Standards in every respect are now lower, from recruit entry to advancement to the most senior ranks in policing. The DEI fuelled narrative of 'bring your whole self to work' now sees officers appear at work with brightly coloured hair, wearing nail polish, makeup, displaying tattoos, chest length beards, and generally looking unprofessional in the eyes of the public. Some forces allow officers to determine which uniform convention to use, by which I mean female officers can now decide to wear conventional male headgear and vice versa. Police officers today often look shabby, unprofessional, and do not reflect the image once associated with a British police officer. This erosion of standards is quite deliberate. It fits nicely with the liberal woke ideology now so embedded within policing and other public sector organisations, that of challenging the conventional narratives, placing the emphasis on the agency of the individual in determining how they should look and dress rather than adhering to conventional organisational standards.

Mediocracy in the guise of progression is now so commonplace that few are any longer surprised when unqualified individuals shoot up the ranks and attain the lofty heights of chief officer status. The eyebrows are being raised less and less. Police response times are woeful, and for non-emergency calls for service, some forces are taking many days to even make contact with the original reporter. Crime detection rates are poor with only 5.6% of reported crimes leading to a person being charged or summonsed. And although some crime categories are indeed on the decline, many more such as serious violence and sexual crime are on the increase. Crime involving the use of knives, especially amongst teenagers, is particularly troubling. And yet the British police service seem unable to up their game. The crime fighting mission, so prevalent in the 1990's when I joined the police, is now a distant memory. Proactive policing has become a thing of the past, no longer will you see officers patrolling on foot on your local high street or shopping centre as a way of preventing crime and engaging with communities. You are now far more likely to see them rushing around in police cars with blue lights flashing as they attend yet another mental health related call. No longer will you be able to call your local police station and chat with a local officer about a problem you are having. Neighbourhood or community policing functions were the first to be slashed when Cameron and May, who's dislike for the police should never be underestimated, removed almost 20,000 frontline police officers in 2010. The service has never recovered from this, albeit I do not assess this factor alone to be at the heart of the issue. Decision-making has been the issue. Decisions taken by chief police officers on what they consider to be strategic priorities, and fighting crime is now sadly far down that list of priorities.

Even in those forces who are under special measures, there is, for the most part, a distinct lack of drive at strategic level to put preventing and detecting crime at the centre of the improvement agenda. Instead, there is lots about organisational re structures, remodelling of systems, budgetary pressures, and 101 other things much easier to discuss than addressing preventing crime and catching criminals. And whilst, yes, some of these issues are certainly organisational interdependencies to effective operational policing, the approach generally seems to be endless internally focussed naval gazing than it does addressing the need for a proper police service for the public. And it is so obvious why this is the case. Many of those sitting around the mahogany boardroom tables in their crisp white shirts and impressive epaulettes have themselves very little in the way of operational exposure. For most, they simply don't know how to get a grip of even the basics of crime prevention and detection. And sadly, given that the service tends to promote in its own image, neither do those in senior positions beneath them. The prophesy is a self-fulfilling one. Appoint enough people to key police leadership positions who lack the necessary technical exposure and competency and when the chips are down, they will predictably fail. They may be able to write an impressive DEI strategy or action plan, be able to talk endlessly about the injustices of underrepresentation in the service and what they plan to do in righting the social wrongs, and discuss the ills of all the misogyny and sexism that pervades policing. However, ask them how to run an effective anti-crime operation and you'll see a load of rabbits in headlights just before you see a cloud of dust as they beat a hasty retreat.

CHAPTER 10

Sir Robert Peel: A Final Word

It is generally best to start at the start, and so it might have seemed more sensible to outline how Peel's 'new police' came into being back in 1829 at the beginning of this book. But I deliberately chose not to do so. I went back just 30 years in my analysis for two reasons; firstly, I wanted to convey what I know from direct personal experience. Yes, I could have quoted others including academics and professional sources and gone back much further in time. But this isn't an academic textbook, more it is designed to be an honest account of what I consider has gone so very wrong in policing. Secondly, I wanted to show just in how short a time, a mere three decades, it has taken things to so radically transform our once iconic British Police service, which, at one point in time whilst difficult to believe now, was the genuine envy of other nations trying to emulate this textbook western democratic style of policing. It is important I feel to close with the father of British policing, Sir Robert Peel, and in doing so demonstrate just how far adrift we have come from Peel's policing mission.

The Peelian Principles

Peel's seminal approach to modern policing structures is best captured in what came to be known as the Peelian Principles. These were the basic tenants which encapsulate the key premise of policing by consent. They in effect reflect the British philosophy of policing and have since been adopted by many countries attempting to emulate this style of democratic policing. In fact, former New York City and Los Angeles police chief, Bill Bratton, described these as his 'bible'. Peel's nine principles are:

1. The basic mission for which the police exist is to prevent crime and disorder
2. The ability of the police to perform their duties is dependent upon public approval of police actions
3. Police must secure the willing co-operation of the public in voluntary observance of the law to be able to secure and maintain the respect of the public
4. The degree of co-operation of the public that can be secured diminishes proportionately to the necessity of the use of physical force
5. Police seek and preserve public favour not by pandering to public opinion but by constantly demonstrating absolute impartial service to the law
6. Police use physical force to the extent necessary to secure observance of the law or to restore order only when the exercise of persuasion, advice and warning is found to be insufficient
7. Police, at all times, should maintain a relationship with the public that gives reality to the historic tradition that the police are the public and the public are the police; the police being only members of the public who are paid to give full-time attention to duties which are incumbent on every citizen in the interests of community welfare and existence
8. Police should always direct their action strictly towards their functions and never appear to usurp the powers of the judiciary
9. The test of police efficiency is the absence of crime and disorder not the visible evidence of police action in dealing with it

It should be immediately evident that Peels' principles remain as relevant today as they were in 1829 when first crafted. Few would argue that these nine policing principles do not reflect what most of the decent law-abiding public continue to expect from its police service. But of concern, is that simultaneously what is also evident is that many of these same principles are now under serious threat. In particular, the first and fifth principles - *that the basic mission for which the police exist is to prevent crime and disorder, and that they seek and preserve public favour not by pandering to public opinion but by constantly demonstrating absolute impartial service to the law* – are particularly relevant to much of what we have discussed here. The maintenance of these principles has seemingly become most challenging and elusive for our contemporary policing structures and of course its leaders. If not careful, and if the current approach is permitted to endure, the entire notion of policing by consent which underpins Peel's philosophy may well be lost forever.

The Way Forward: A Factory Reset?

I have described here much of what I consider has gone wrong with our police over the last three decades, and it is obvious, to me at least, just how much needs to change to get the profession back on track. I've often described this as the need to perform a complete factory reset, so significant are the issues and solutions required to resolve them that nothing less than a full reset will achieve the change and the necessary measures to restore public trust and confidence. There have been many reviews into British policing, some of which have suggested sensible reform. But policing remains the favourite toy of politicians, and so reforms made to the profession, rather than be strategically focussed or long-term in nature tend to give way to the short-term populist knee-jerks, some of which we have discussed here; changes to the police educational framework and the disciplinary processes being two such recent examples. These are not strategic in nature but are instead 'reforms' for the sake of achieving quick wins and placating one side or the other. Rather, the police service needs a root and branch review, with a genuine desire and commitment to achieve the reforms required. Previous governments and Home

Secretaries have failed to grasp this opportunity, instead tinkering at the edges of policing but achieving very little meaningful or positive change in the process. Something akin to a Royal Commission is required, a process that will forensically examine policing in its entirety. Key to this will be defining the mission of the police, to properly outline and define its role and functions, and just as crucially to explicitly state those roles it should not be undertaking. Standards of recruitment, educational accreditations, and promotion standards along with remuneration should all be on the table. Only when considering these issues together will policing be able to achieve the much-needed factory reset, and to get back to the business once again of providing a proper public service, of preventing and detecting crime. Amongst these reforms must be the reinstatement of Peel's principles, of the original philosophical framework, in my view as relevant today as they were when Peel crafted them. Critically, it must be crystal clear that policing should no longer indulge itself in social causes or in virtue signalling activity. It must be completely neutral of such issues. DEI agendas, if required at all, must be appropriate, proportionate, and lawful, they must be truly inclusive and the pathological obsession with equity - equality of outcome rather than of opportunity -must cease. Then, and only then, will policing be able to restore its key mission: take care of the good people and lock up the bad. And society will be all the better for it.

The End

Afterword

It has taken me some time to sit down and write this book, and it has been something of an emotional journey. I have written it during some personal challenges, and as I navigate my way into retirement and onto the next chapter after 31 years as a policeman. For the most part, I will treasure my time in policing, and to see the profession experience such a decline in recent years has been heart-breaking. Doubtless too, as I have written, I realise that in some ways I may even have been part of this terrible decline, if not actively then certainly by association, especially as a former senior leader in the service myself. I thought that writing a little about my career and the problems which I assess need to be resolved in policing would have provided something of a cathartic outlet, but that could not be further from the truth. If anything, mapping it out like this shows how far the British police service has fallen, and so how far we must climb to restore it. That is a journey I will now sadly not be part of, but it is one that I certainly wish to see happen. Despite what some may think, I did not write this book to make money, to settle scores, or as an exercise in self-indulgence. I wrote it as my frustration had become so great that I could no longer resist the impulse to tell my story. Some may take issue with my analysis, whilst others may agree with it; either way is fine. We still live in a democratic society and disagreement and debate are healthy and necessary aspects of that. If anyone has taken offence at any aspect of what I have written here, I offer not one ounce of apology. Remember, offence is almost always taken, not given.

The principle audience of this telling are those who might not have been previously aware of the issues I have described. It is my sincere hope that some may find even a shred of enlightenment here, and hopefully perhaps even a little entertainment. I have at all times tried to be honest and balanced in my analysis, to be respectful, and to acknowledge that there remain some very good things about British policing. The opinions expressed here are mine; they are my opinion and my analysis only. They do not represent the views of anyone else, nor of any other organisation. Lastly, in no way do I decry those at the front end of the profession, most of whom do an excellent job despite the pressures they face. It is to these selfless, hardworking public servants that I dedicate this book. Keep doing what you do, look after one another, and keep faith that things will get better. Policing is still the best job on the planet.

February 2024

Printed in Great Britain
by Amazon